The Holy Triangle

JOEL NEDERHOOD

BAKER BOOK HOUSE
GRAND RAPIDS, MICHIGAN

Foreword

Few would deny that we are in the throes of a grave crisis in personal morality. Even those who attempt to justify some of the modern deviations by developing new theories of personal conduct admit that few have the sense to use the new theories profitably. Marriage today is in a state of grave decay. And this of course is just an extension of the same degeneracy that sends millions to movies rated "X" and floods the stage with drama that depicts the basest level of human interest.

The moral crisis of our age is so staggering because no class of people has been left untouched. Clergymen and others to whom confused people divulge their twisted thoughts and emotions often remark that apparently there is no segment of society that has not been corrupted by the rapid decay of moral insight. Even those who ordinarily are expected to give leadership in exemplary living are stumbling over their own sexuality today. The disillusionment that results gradually erodes the ideals of others and the big slide into moral chaos accelerates.

The chapters of this book are brief examinations of marriage, the home, the responsibilities of parents, sexual love, abortion, and other matters that affect us all so deeply — an examination of these in the light of the Bible, the Word of God. The present shambles in our lives should be proof enough that we must now go back to this great book and listen obediently to its pointed instruction. Those who refuse, call down upon themselves the emptiness and ashes that finally comes into the lives of those who reject the help God offers.

When it comes to our moral lives the choices are very simple, really. Either a man listens to God and does His will or he walks the road of selfishness. The road of selfishness is very appealing, very appealing indeed. But it leads, as the saying goes, to destruction.

It is my fervent hope that the chapters that follow will help you walk the other road. For those who are determined to learn the will of the Lord and do it can expect unlimited power from God Himself. Jesus, His only begotten Son, died on Calvary so that He could bring forgiveness to all who believe in Him and so that He could send His Holy Spirit into their lives to help them live with purity and chastity even in this disobedient and perverse generation.

JOEL NEDERHOOD

Contents

1

The Holy Triangle

Most people have heard of a marriage triangle. We speak about a triangle in connection with marriage when, beside the husband and wife, there is a third party who woos either the husband away from his wife or the wife away from her husband. Sometimes that third party can be very serious about his intentions. He deliberately plans to destroy the existing marriage so that he himself can marry the wife. Sometimes the third party is just frivolous and flirtatious. He weakens the marriage by having his fun, but he doesn't really want to destroy it. Whatever the case may be, when it comes to marriage, there is no room for a third party. Triangles usually spell the death of marriage.

That is very important to remember because all of us are in trouble when the institution of marriage is in trouble. Individuals suffer — there are not many frustrations and bitternesses more shattering than those experienced within a marriage that has gone sour. And the children, poor children, think of what they go through when Mother and Dad become enemies. It scars the children for the rest of their lives and often their marriages suffer too.

That is why marriage triangles are so damaging. When someone on the outside insinuates his selfish desire into a marriage situation there is no end to the devastation that is caused. Today this kind of devastation is occurring on a very wide scale. In some countries of course, divorce is practically impossible. But that doesn't mean that all the marriages are robustly healthy. Often the opposite is the case. In such countries, concubinage and other forms of adultery take the place of divorce. Where divorces are relatively easy to acquire, however, marriages are dissolved very frequently, often because a third party is in the picture, or because one of the marriage partners wants the freedom to look for a third party. According to a national newsmagazine in the United States, one out of every two marriages in the state of California ends up in the divorce courts. Imagine: one out of every two! Within the American nation as a whole there have been around 400,000 divorces a year since World War II.

Now it's not difficult to imagine the kind of trouble that causes. If you have 350,000 or 380,000 divorces a year in a country, that's 700,000 or 800,000 people involved if you take the parties in the divorce alone. Right now 20 percent of the population in the United States is directly involved in the widespread collapse of marriage. So if you are getting married or are celebrating your anniversary, are you doing anything to insure the future of your marriage? Even if this year marks your fifth, or tenth, or twentieth anniversary? Teen-agers are not the only ones whose marriages break up, you know. In the United States 40 percent of all broken marriages have lasted ten years or more. Thirteen percent survived more than twenty years before the break came.

Is there anything that can absolutely guarantee the stability of a marriage? Yes there is. It's a special kind of marriage triangle. A triangle? A third party to a marriage that can make it last? You have just read that triangles generally destroy marriages. That is true of ordinary triangles that consist of a husband and a wife and a third party who tries to get the wife away from her husband or the husband away from the wife. But there is another kind of triangle, a holy one, that can give a marriage a foundation that will insure that nothing short of death itself will destroy it. What kind of a triangle is that? It is the marriage of a husband and wife who live their lives, both of them, in fellowship with Jesus Christ — in fellowship with God. That kind of triangle, a husband and wife and their common Savior, is permanent — as permanent as any human relationship can ever be.

It is true of course, that the marriages of many whose Christianity is formal do collapse. That is bound to happen because a formal Christianity will not help preserve marriage. The ills that weaken marriage to-day can be cured only with the strong medicine of a living faith in a living Christ who is always present in the husband's life and in the life of his wife. People who have made the common mistake of assuming that their religion consists only in that which they do in church and who have failed to take their Savior into every room in their homes will not find the assistance they must have if their marriages are going to survive. Jesus is not embarrassed by the realities of the home and marriage. He is the Lord of all life: the Lord of the factory, the museum, the kitchen and the hearth, and of the marriage bed. And that husband and wife who both confess every moment that Christ is the sovereign Lord of everything they do, possess a guar-antee that their marriage will not be terminated by the whims and sins of one of them.

Jesus affirmed His interest in the marriages of His people by choosing to begin His ministry of miracles at a marriage celebration. In the Gospel according to John, the first verses of the second chapter begin with this prosaic statement: "On the third day there was a marriage at Cana of Galilee; and the mother of Jesus was there; Jesus was also invited to the marriage, with his disciples." The chapter then goes on to tell how Jesus contributed to the success of that marriage celebration. This is amazing when you stop to think about it because just a few verses before this, in the first chapter of John, we encounter a religious truth of the most exalted kind. We read, for example, "In the beginning was the Word, and the Word was with God, and the Word was God" (v. 1). We also read, "And the Word became flesh and dwelt among us, full of grace and truth; we have beheld his glory, glory as of the only Son from the Father" (v. 14). Now that is real religion, isn't it? But just a few verses further, we read about this marriage in Cana. Marriages are actually very ordinary human events.

That is the way the Bible is. The realities of the Christian revelation are carried right down to the ground floor of common human experience. Thus we find Jesus Christ, the only begotten Son of God, the "Word become flesh," at a wedding. That was not an accident. It wasn't a happenstance. The life of Christ advanced according to plan. From His birth to His ascension, every event of His life contributed to His redemptive accomplishment. And the fact that He went to a wedding is an announcement that He wants to go to yours if you are not married now, and, if you are, He wants to be the third party in a holy triangle that will insure the permanence and significance of your marriage.

Well, what can Jesus do for you and for your marriage? The first thing He can do for you is this: He

10

can help you understand the holy significance of the marriage state. Let us be honest with one another: marriage today is despised. You and I have heard influential radio and TV personalities say, "Monogamous marriage — one man, one woman, 'till death do us part' — just isn't realistic anymore." People talk about trial marriages and nonstructured relationships. Or they throw monogamy overboard for serial polygamy, for the law prohibits their having more than one wife at one time. Marriage is an old worn-out convention that is left over from our prudish past. It still serves some people well, but millions today go their own sweet way, and do as they please.

That is why so many marriages collapse. Is it any wonder so many of our starry-eyed young people who get married in June are ready to call it quits when September comes? If a marriage is built on nothing more than the passing emotions of the husband and wife, come some gray Monday, the bottom is going to drop out of that marriage, do what you will. How *can* it last, if that's all it's built on?

But if a husband and a wife believe in Jesus Christ and if the greatest desire of their lives is to serve Him, Jesus will show them that their marriage is fine and wonderful. He will do that as they listen together to His holy Word with obedience. Within that Word, Jesus speaks about marriage often and clearly.

Marriage is not just a naturalistic event that can be explained wholly in terms of the wishes and needs of the two marriage partners. But it is God's ordinance. The husband and the wife become one flesh. Marriage is a mysterious ordinance which God in His mercy has bestowed upon the human family.

You may not tamper with an institution like that. If you have vowed before God to live with your mate

11

in the institution of marriage, you must now look upon that state as an exalted, sacred aspect of your life. But you can feel this way about marriage only when your understanding of marriage flows from a living faith in the Lord Jesus Christ.

So then, if you and your husband, or you and your wife, whatever the case may be, know that this Jesus is your Savior and Lord, He will give you a priceless insight into the true mystery of the marriage state.

But Christ does still more for marriage partners who believe in Him. Through their faith in His Word, they understand the real significance of marriage. Christ also provides His people with resources that qualify them to do His will. In connection with marriage, this means that Christ provides those who live within the discipline of the marriage bond the grace they need in order to make their marriages successful.

There are many, many problems connected with marriage, of course. Some of them are not too serious: just ordinary disagreements and momentary displays of anger. Some are terribly serious. People can find out, after they live together, that there are certain subjects that cause trouble every time they are mentioned. There are problems related to sexual adjustment. There are problems related to the birth and nurture of children. There are problems related to money. Sometimes marriages can become ongoing battles. There are decisions that have to be made. The husband's career has to be advanced. People have to move from one place to another. And so it goes, on and on and on. That is the way life is — for everybody, without exception.

Christ gives His people the grace to go through these things together and to face them in His power. They make mistakes, of course. They offend each other. But when these mistakes are made and the offenses occur, they are able to receive one another with forgiveness because Christ teaches them how to forgive one another without limitation. This keeps deep-seated resentments from building up. When the big crises come, such a husband and wife will find themselves together in prayer asking for help. Christ goes with them through the crises of their own making, those caused by the deficiencies of their own personalities. He is also with them in the dark moments of life when tragedy strikes. When sickness and disease drop their cloak of gloom, and death starts fountains of tears, Christ is there.

No wonder so many marriages collapse today. People just do not have the moral stamina to carry on when the ordinary problems that are a part of marriage break their hearts. Unless you have the power of the living Christ in your soul, you will be crushed by the harsh realities that cannot be escaped within a normal marriage.

Yes, it is true, there is a holy triangle that can make a marriage beautiful and lasting. It comes into existence when both marriage partners believe in Jesus Christ and determine to live each day in His service. That triangle insures that the marriage will not be broken by a third party who tries to alienate the affections of one of the partners, for the living Christ will help the partners to live together in faithfulness and love. Marriage partners who together acknowledge that they are partners with Jesus Christ understand the holiness of the institution of marriage itself and often marvel at its mystery. A husband and wife who both believe in Jesus Christ will discover that Jesus will enable them to bear their most terrible burden and, in the darkest hour, He will reveal the glory of His light.

13

Perhaps you are contemplating marriage. What kind of a marriage will it be? Will it consist of just you and your fiance, just you two alone, no one else? If that is true, there's a rocky road ahead. It is even possible that your marriage will not last very long. Perhaps you are a Christian yourself, but the person you are going to marry is not. That is not very wise either. If there are two people who are married, but only one of them is looking to Christ, the sacred triangle will not exist. One of its sides will be missing. Have you really considered what you are getting yourself into, if you claim to be a believer in Christ, but you are going to marry someone who is not? You are making a very grave mistake.

Or it may be that you have been married for some time already, but your marriage is not really a part of a holy triangle at all. It is just you and your mate, just you two, with no faith in Jesus. You never read the Bible together. You don't know what it is to pray together. You have never been able to give your children any religious guidance, because you are at sea yourself. Naturally, sometimes things get pretty black for you.

Have you really considered what Christ offers men and women in connection with their marriages? He died on Calvary's cross so that all who believe on Him can experience His redemption. That redemption can be yours if you repent of your own sin and rebellion and believe that Jesus Christ is God's only begotten Son who died so that believers might have abundant life.

Husband, wife, believe on this Christ, and His perfect love will make yours last until the Savior summons you to be with Him forever.

2

Leaving and Cleaving

"Tell me, Charles, what is it about your present wife that makes you so enthusiastic about her? After all, you've been around and you have been married twice before, and now you are so in love with Madeline. . . . How come? I know it's a bit personal, but won't you tell us?"

It was a radio interviewer who asked the question, and he was speaking to a prominent television personalitly. Of course, the names used are fictitious, but the question is not. It was asked publicly — over the radio. It was answered publicly too. The television star was entirely matter-of-fact as he described the superior virtues of his latest wife. The interviewer and actor talked about this fascinating subject a little while longer. There was no apology; there was not the slightest trace of shame. They acted as if their attitudes were entirely wholesome and very common.

Unfortunately, the attitudes expressed in that radio interview *are* very common. They are common precisely because so many well-known people brazenly despise marriage and batter away at the foundations of society and of a moral world. The television actor who gloated publicly over his good fortune in having secured so fine a third wife, is a principle star of a prime television show designed to entertain the whole family. Young children and teen-agers watch it along with their parents. Don't underestimate the influence of a man like that. Because of the public actions and statements of prominent people in business, politics, and entertainment, millions of impressionable young people cannot help but think that marriage is a lark and a joke.

This is the reason why the subject of marriage has become, in many respects, a very gloomy subject. It is getting harder and harder for all the glamour and fantasy associated with marriage to hide the undeniable fact that marriage, it sometimes seems, brings more sorrow than joy. The bride may look radiant, and her gown may be out of this world. The bridesmaids may be stunning, and the little flower girl and ring bearer both cute and charming. The groom and his men may be handsome and cool. And afterward the whole party may roar off in the finest car they can find. But none of this destroys the fact that, frequently within a few months, many of these same newlyweds are among the most unhappy people in the world.

Often they are divorced quite soon, or they try separation for a while and are divorced a little later. You have to give some of them credit for trying to make the best of it, but they begin a weary round of quarreling and bickering that becomes their normal way of life. Often husband and wife become arch-enemies, competitors who delight in inflicting suffering upon one another. They suffer and their children suffer, and nothing ever seems to break the monotony of their life-long battle.

The institution of marriage is in deep trouble today. Why? Because an overwhelming majority of young people getting married do not have the slightest idea what they are getting into. Their total development prior to marriage has not prepared them for the often

16

harsh realities of marriage, the day-by-day activities and decisions that accompany living together.

Handling money, for example, is a frequent cause of disagreement that causes many marriages to collapse. Yet young people often enter marriage before they have had an opportunity to develop sensible, responsible habits of handling money.

Moreover, modern culture does not prepare young people for the tensions that are naturally a part of the marriage relationship. From the very beginning, new husbands and wives discover that there is a lot more to living together than they every dreamed of when they were rubbing sun tan oil on each other's backs. The arrival of children complicates marriages, often almost unbearably. It takes a high level of maturity to meet the demands of marriage, and a high percentage of those being married today just don't have it.

Yes, in certain respects, many couples are no more prepared for marriage when they approach the altar than they were when they were ten years old. Oh, they are mature enough physically, and they know a great deal about the physical aspects of marriage. But they do not really know what *marriage* is, and they do not realize how it will change their lives. They do not know what marriage is *for* either. They are ignorant because they seldom hear God's message concerning marriage. If your understanding of marriage is formed in isolation from God's message, you are bound to have trouble.

Jesus, God's Son, talked about marriage while on earth. Once, when men asked Him about divorce, He ruled divorce out of the question by saying: ". . . Have you not read that he who made them from the beginning made them male and female, and said, For this reason a man shall leave his father and mother, and be joined to his wife, and the two shall become one? So they are no longer two but one. What therefore God has joined together, let not man put asunder" (Matthew 19:4-6). These words provide us with a fundamental insight into the Biblical view of marriage. This passage indicates that the Bible is a very practical book. We must pay attention to it as we prepare for marriage and as we discharge our responsibilities within the marriage state.

From Jesus' words concerning marriage, we learn, first of all, that marriage involves *leaving*. Marriage is an entirely new way of life that makes it necessary to leave your old way of life behind. We must leave the family into which we were born in order to start another, new family. This must be done in spite of the fact that family relationships, ideally, are some of the most intimate there are. Children develop strong dependence upon their parents, and parents become dependent upon their children too. This was true in Jesus' day as well. Yet when He described marriage, Jesus went back to the oldest description of it we find in the Bible — the original of His words is found in Genesis 2 — and He said that marriage means leaving father and mother.

When young people are married, they should no longer feel dependent upon their parents. This doesn't mean that parents may not help their married children when emergencies arise. But if a man cannot stand on his own feet and earn his own living and make decisions for himself, he is not yet ready for marriage. If this is true with respect to one's father and mother, it is also true with respect to other social relationships people have before they are married. They must leave their families, and the old gang too, and the crowd they used to run with.

18

Couples not emotionally capable of making this kind of break with their old way of life, or unwilling to make this kind of break, will face many problems. Every marriage counselor, every minister, everyone who deals with unhappy people whose marriages are collapsing will tell you that one of the most frequent reasons for the collapse is this: either husband or wife, or both, have never left home, or they have never really cut their ties with their old gang. They think marriage is simply rooming together legally, while they continue living as before. Many marriages fail because the partners didn't realize that they were supposed to be on their own.

Jesus also says that marriage involves *joining*. The King James version of the Bible used the word *cleaving*. That is a quaint, old-fashioned word, but it expresses very nicely another important aspect of marriage that must be understood if your marriage is going to be a happy one. Cleaving is clinging; to cleave is to cling. In an ideal marriage the husband and wife cling to one another, not in desperation, but in the calm assurance that God wants them to face life together. They engage in the exciting business of living jointly; they live as if they were really one.

How many young couples never actually understand this aspect of marriage! Perhaps you have never really understood that God wants you and your marriage partner to be one in your basic ideas and ideals; He wants you to be united as you work together and pray together and live together. This, of course, would be impossible if you were not compatible in your religious life — yet there are thousands of people who try marriage even when there is no religious compatibility whatever.

The absurdity of mixed marriage is aptly described

by the late Dr. Peter Eldersveld, who at the time was radio minister of the Christian Reformed Church. He said, "Suppose you are a young man who lives in Chicago, and you decide to make a trip to San Francisco. So you go down to Union Station and purchase a ticket on the train. Waiting in the same line with you at the window is a very attractive young lady. She is going some place too, and, as boys will do, you find an excuse to strike up a conversation with her, in the course of which you ask; 'Where are you going?' 'I'm going to New York,' she says. 'Well, isn't that wonderful!' you say, 'I'm going to San Francisco; so let's travel together on the same train, shall we?' Now if she is a fairly intelligent girl, she will immediately begin to doubt your sanity, unless, of course, you are joking. But obviously you are not joking; you are serious. And so you try to persuade her that this is a perfectly reasonable thing to do. And suppose that she begins to agree with you, and so you finally persuade each other that this thing can really be done. Well, that's absurd, isn't it? It simply is out of the question. The whole story is ridiculous.

"But this is what thousands of young people are doing with their marriages."

Yes, when people who do not share the same religious convictions still marry one another, it is like two people with totally different destinations who try to travel on the same train or the same plane. This happens because today, most people seem to think that the only real union found in marriage is a physical union. For the rest, they want to go their own separate ways. What a terrible mistake! You know how it is then: they each have their own career, their own bank account, and even their own car. They are incensed if anyone suggests for a minute that they may not do

20

as they please, even if their pleasure involves questionable relationships with other married or single people. The only time they are willing to consider themselves one is when doing so gives them a tax advantage.

Jesus says that marriage is a union in which husband and wife cleave to one another and become one — a social unit that responds to life efficiently and well. This does not mean that there are never circumstances in which husband and wife will not have their own job and even have different interests. But basically they are on the same side, they are on the same team, working together for the same purposes and goals. No circumstance short of death can separate them.

Marriage, then, according to Jesus, involves leaving and cleaving. Obviously, marriage demands a great deal of maturity. This is the reason so many teen-age marriages end in failure. It takes maturity to leave your father and your mother and destroy your dependence upon former associates. Two people must be really grown up before they are able to forsake all others and cleave to each other. But today there are thousands of young people who are getting married in spite of the fact that they have never really grown up. They are unwilling to make the break necessary and to abandon their old way of life, and they are unwilling to make the sacrifices necessary as they begin their new life together. That is why they weep so much and frustration as bitter as ashes destroys their joy.

What can be done about the sad state of modern marriage? Practically everyone who knows about the problem will tell you that our culture needs some preventive medicine very badly if there is going to be progress in healing this widespread social disease. When two immature people marry, their problems become a hundred times worse than they would have been if they had understood the meaning of marriage while they were still single. The preventive approach to this problem, fortunately, is being recognized, and over the last thirty years, marriage preparation courses have been started in some seven hundred colleges and universities in the United States. Some school systems have inaugurated a series of courses, running from nursery through high school, that deal with family relationships. These might do some good. But nothing is really going to do much good until we begin to teach our children what marriage actually is — right within our homes.

Maybe it is necessary, finally, for parents to declare war against any influence that comes into the lives of their children and undercuts the Christian view of marriage. We must realize that everything that makes marriage look like a farce contributes to the destruction of our nation's homes. When we laugh with our children at the television programs that make husbands look like clowns and family life like a comedy of errors, we should understand that the devil himself may well have the last laugh. If we allow our growing youngsters to soak up the sensational immoral fare that dominates the movie industry and corrupts respectable book stores, they are not going to be equipped to respond properly to the demands a Christian marriage will make of them.

You'll be unpopular for a little while if you prohibit your children from watching certain television programs, and they will not like it if you tell them they may not go to this or that movie or read certain books. But in the long run they will realize that you are doing them a favor. And, incidentally, you will enjoy your grandchildren a lot more, if you are willing to take a stand today.

Of course, you can only do things like this if your children realize that you are doing them because you want your family to be dominated by Christ's influence. Otherwise they will think you are a tyrant. They must know that you want them to know the Bible's message about life and the Bible's message about marriage. We must give our children the message of the Word of God. They must grow up with it. They must get to the point where everything they say and do will be done in the light of the Bible. They must know the Bible's view of the home and of marriage. They must know the Bible's condemnation of immorality and un-chastity. They must know that they are living their lives every day beneath the eye of the Judge of all the earth, and they must serve Him.

Then, when someday they start looking for someone to marry, they will remember Jesus, too. They will not make the awful mistake of marrying someone who doesn't care at all about the Savior. They will know the duties and the joys of marriage as the Bible de-scribes them, and so they will be able to leave you and to cleave to their marriage partner. And you will be able to let them go as you must, because you will be able to commit them to the Lord.

But perhaps you are one of those who feels that he will never be able to give his children the Christian view of marriage because you are all too aware that your own marriage has deteriorated so badly. You know that you will never be capable of teaching your children what a Christian marriage is, because your own is so unchristian. As you look at your marriage in the light of what the Bible says marriage must be, you sense at once that you have failed God. You are ab-

23

solutely right when you assume that you cannot teach your children what a Christian marriage is unless you can show them what it is in your own life. Is there anything you can do about your problem?

First of all, you must remember that God does not describe what Christian marriage is without providing people with the power and the grace they will need in order to make their marriages more Christian. You and your wife, or you and your husband, must recognize the depths of your own problem very frankly and you must repent of your sin and confess Jesus Christ as your Savior. Maybe you just don't love each other anymore. You could love each other again if you would both become believers, if you would become brother and sister in the Lord, for then you would understand that the love that must exist in marriage must transcend our daily irritations. It is a love that exists in spite of the many, many problems that are a part of every marriage.

As Jesus Christ performed His first miracle at a marriage feast, He still performs His miracles as He sanctifies Christian marriages and makes them happy and wonderful. Has Christ performed His miracle for you? Christ will save your marriage if you confess your sin and flee to Him for salvation.

3

Is Marriage Obsolete?

Is marriage obsolete? How would you answer that question? Many people evidently think marriage is through as a useful social institution. There are several recent developments that suggest that thousands are ready to give up on this time-honored social structure which most of us have generally considered one of the foundations of human society. Several factors contribute to this growing consensus that marriage is fast losing its usefulness, and anyone who is concerned about his own future, the future of his children, and the future of his country should be well aware of them.

The first factor is the pill. The Pill — let's spell that with a capital "P" — the Pill is revolutionizing society. The Pill is accepted today as a normal part of our lives. Many people believe that it has made marriage obsolete by removing from marriage one of its most useful functions: marriage is no longer necessary for making sex legitimate. So long as there was fear that there would be offspring, casual relations between men and women were not without risk. Today that risk is gone.

Who knows how many people are taking advantage of the new situation? Many college students are, and you cannot really blame them, because they are encouraged to use the birth control materials that are available. Dr. Joseph Fletcher, a professor of Christian ethics, has suggested colleges should offer birth control services to unmarried students along with other health services. He said, "They ought to be regarded as a medical resource owed to the student as needed and requested." It is no secret anymore that there are many couples on our campuses who are living together in what is called an "unstructured relationship." Dr. David Powelson, associated with the health service of a large university, has said that these "unstructured relationships" may be the shape of the future. He says, "Stable, open, non-marital relationships are pushing the border of what society is going to face in ten years."

One newsmagazine has stated that those who believe that marriage is worthwhile seem to be a vanishing breed because of "the new morality of premarital cohabitation on campuses, uninhibited extramarital liaisons, and divorce rates climbing even for vintage marriages. . . ." It added that "the whole drift of contemporary history from the technology of the pill to the secularization of existing institutions" seems to oppose those who continue to hold a traditional view of marriage and its value.

In his book, *The World of the Formerly Married,* Morton M. Hunt provides evidence that many people who have been divorced have their own kind of "unstructured relationships." It's all a part of the big picture of the new world men are creating in which sex and marriage need not be united.

Another factor that contributes to the growing consensus that marriage is obsolete is the increased interest in homosexual and other unnatural relationships, a trend that should not be overlooked. The forces that are destroying marriage are often sordid and perhaps we prefer not to notice them. But they are there and they are strong and they are aiming their destructive power at the center of the marriage relationship.

Dr. Mary Calderone of the Sex Information and Educational Council of the United States illustrated the new point of view when she announced that it was the general view of the psychiatrists, sociologists, clergymen, and businessmen on the SIECUS board that "homosexuality can be as constructive as marriage can be destructive." Perhaps reluctantly, but of necessity, we must recognize that she is raising prophetic questions when she asks, "People don't have to marry today to get a housekeeper, or for sex — so what do we marry for? Shall we have marriage in twenty-five years?" In the degree that such opinions become more widespread, marriage will be considered an unnecessarily restrictive kind of social relationship.

Finally, one of the most potent factors that contributes to the growing consensus that marriage is obsolete is this: Religious leaders are inclined to agree that this is so. "You shall not commit adultery" is fast becoming "Perhaps you had better not commit adultery," and is on the way toward becoming, "It doesn't make much difference whether you do or not, so long as you don't hurt anyone." For example, the British Council of Churches commissioned a study committee to prepare a case for the traditional Christian view of premarital abstinence "and faithfulness within marriage." The publication of this committee did nothing of the kind. Happily, their final statement did not bear the approval of the British Council. In the popular mind, however, the statement can hardly be divorced from the church, and, of course, there were clergymen engaged in the study. This report denies that there can be any set rules regarding abstinence outside marriage and faithfulness within. It says, "Intelligent Christian opinion no longer regards the Bible, or even the New Testament, as a textbook from which one can extract authoritative rulings, which automatically decide contemporary problems."

Each of these, in its own way, contributes to the growing feeling that marriage is no longer very useful: the Pill, new attitudes toward homosexuality, and the unhelpful statements of certain religious leaders. Many people have consciously concluded that marriage is a thing of the past, but far more have concluded this unconsciously. Rising divorce rates, widespread promiscuity, and high incidence of unnatural relationships are proof of how sex and marriage have been put asunder in the common mind. Most likely you have been influenced by this too, in some degree or another. Maybe you are a teen-ager or a college student. Or you may be a person who is married now but doesn't consider this marriage permanent. If you don't understand the meaning and usefulness of marriage, you are bound to have serious trouble. Marriage is not nor will it ever be obsolete, and if you suspect it is, you should pay close attention to what the Bible says about it. In spite of the false statements some people are spreading around — that the Bible has nothing to say about problems like these — the Bible has a great deal to say, and you and I must listen.

There is nothing mysterious nor ambiguous in the Bible's clear support of the institution of marriage. The Old Testament commandment, "You shall not commit adultery," is familiar to many. But that is only part of the story. Leviticus, one of the Old Testament books, contains explicit laws that governed the families of the Israelites, and many of them were designed to insure that family life remained pure and undefiled. The destruction of Sodom and Gomorrah, recorded in Genesis 19, is a clear demonstration of God's hatred of unnatural sexual relationships. There should be no question that the Old Testament condemns all sexual relationships that occur outside of the institution of marriage.

The New Testament also prohibits promiscuity and impurity of every kind. In I Corinthians 6:18, the Bible says, "Shun immorality. . . ." You may not even *consider* it. When possibilities for it occur you must turn your back and run as fast as you can in the other direction. You know what immorality is. It is precisely the kind of loose sexual conduct that is so prevalent today and which is even supported sometimes by men who claim to be religious leaders. But the Bible does not support it. All the modern talk about the legitimacy of immorality and adultery is diametrically opposed to the Bible's clear-cut message.

Do you know why immorality is so dangerous? It is because those who live in it put their immortal souls in jeopardy. In verse 9 of this same chapter we are told, "Do you not know that the unrighteous will not inherit the kingdom of God? Do not be deceived; neither the immoral nor idolaters, nor adulterers nor homosexuals . . . will inherit the kingdom of God." You had better think about that, if you are one of those who has been deceived by the modern nonsense that is being circulated, if you have been taken in by foolishness that declares that it doesn't make any difference what you do with your body, as long as you don't hurt anyone. Now you know that the Bible says that those who persist in this kind of rebellion against the law of God "will not inherit the kingdom of God."

The Bible does not talk this way about immorality and adultery because it views sex as something unworthy and essentially impure. In Genesis 1:27 we read that man was created in the image of God, and immediately the Bible adds, "male and female he created them." The sexuality of man is related to his ability to reflect God's image and, therefore, the Bible maintains a realistic and exalted view of these characteristics of man throughout. Don't refuse to consider the Bible's ideas concerning these matters just because you think them prudish or Victorian. The Bible is way ahead of the licentious theories that prevail today. They are essentially naturalistic and primitive. But the Bible recognizes man's real humanity and spirituality and always emphasizes that he is an image-bearer of God.

Because you are not a beast, the fullness of your humanity is expressed in the quality of the relationships you have with other people. The sexual problem cannot be described in terms of short term satisfactions but must be described in terms of its effect upon essential human relationships. Therefore, God has carefully circumscribed this area of human activity and He has declared that sexual relationships can contribute to personal well-being and the well-being of society only when they occur within the institution of marriage. If you engage in such relationships outside the realm of your marriage, you disqualify yourself as a friend of God. God calls you to shun immorality and to flee to Him asking His forgiveness and receiving His redemption.

Marriage is not, nor will it ever be obsolete because it is an institution of God, and it has been ordained in order that the sexual aspects of human life may be expressed properly and usefully. Today we are entering into a new era in which men will have to see the spiritual foundation of marriage before they will be willing to live chastely and purely with one another and before God. It used to be that the usefulness of marriage was accepted by all men because marriage was necessary in order to make children legitimate, homosexuality was frowned upon, and the broad power of ecclesiastical authority fortified marriage. Now that these conditions no longer prevail, the only justification for marriage is a justification which arises from an understanding of the Bible and of the significance of Jesus Christ. The need for marriage today can be felt only by those who sincerely want to honor God with every aspect of their lives. Marriage provides man, who is a sexual being, the possibility of purity. If you are not interested in honoring God, there is not much you can do to resist the overwhelming degradation of marriage in this present age.

The moral depravity of this age, an age which seriously questions the very necessity of marriage itself, an age which pursues its wanton pleasures without regard for the will of God, demonstrates how essential it is for men and women to be united to Jesus Christ by faith. Some years ago a semblance of moral sensitivity was preserved by legal statements proclaimed either by the church or by the state. Today we see that legalistic approaches to moral problems are doomed to bankruptcy. Law can never redeem mankind, for it is capable only of describing proper conduct. And today we need so much more than a description of what is right; we need the power to *do* it. Therefore, the Bible that counsels men to shun immorality does so by relating this flight from impurity to Christ, and to faith in Him. Outside of Christ there is no real possibility anymore for truly moral action. Thank God, there still remains some feeling for what is genuinely good in human conduct, but this is the dwindling heritage of a past that is being repudiated. The "unstructured relationships" found on campus and within other sectors of our society are the harbingers of a bleak future in which the family will be destroyed and human sexuality will be expressed in unwholesome and perverted ways.

The Bible therefore calls you to a moral, God-honoring life that grows out of an understanding that you are not your own, but you belong to Jesus Christ. This is the context in which God's commandment, "Shun immorality . . . ," is found: "Shun immorality. Every other sin which a man commits is outside the body; but the immoral man sins against his own body. Do you not know that your body is a temple of the Holy Spirit within you, which you have from God? You are not your own; you were bought with a price. So glorify God in your body."

It is not strange that many today are beginning to feel that marriage is a passing social structure, and man must learn to use his new freedom in new ways. This is the logical conclusion of the naturalistic view of man that prevails today. Short term satisfaction and easy adjustments to immediate needs become the only worthwhile goals in human conduct. Anything that inhibits men and women and frustrates them must be removed one way or another. Therefore sexual conduct becomes just another area of experimentation so that the greatest happiness may be achieved.

The result of this approach to moral problems is chaos, and ultimately we must expect utter ruin. Dr. Lloyd J. Averill is an educator who takes issue with the prevalent looseness of this age. Writing an article entitled, "Sexuality in Crisis," he has stated: "I would suggest that our frankness about sex in this generation is a sign of our chaos, of a world in which our human connections are in a state of serious disorganization, a world in which little that is really human is left. We have talked openly about sex in a desperate attempt to bring order out of chaos, to recover our humanity. But we have engaged in a misplaced frankness, and the result is a deepened crisis."

Dr. Averill is right. There is a crisis today in connection with the most intimate of all human relationships. The extent of the crisis is measured in the way marriage itself is disparaged and a wide variety of free relationships are condoned and in some instances encouraged. If you are one of those whose life is being torn apart by this present crisis, God tells you now to shun immorality and to flee to Jesus Christ. If you are one of those who has been taken in by demonic suggestions that you can do with your body what you please, then you are contributing to the final disorganization of human life, the dehumanization of man himself, and, if you don't repent of your sin, you are now insuring your own eternal experience of God's rejection.

Don't listen to those who speak so persuasively about a new liberty which allows men and women to enter all kinds of intimate relationships with all sorts of people. Marriage remains God's meaningful provision in which men and women are given an opportunity to enjoy the fulness of their life together. Shun immorality, whoever you are, and flee to Jesus Christ. Confess your sin, confess that He is your Savior, and ask Him to give you the strength to live according to His will. He will give you the gift of purity. And that's what you really want, down deep, isn't it?

4

Marriage Is for Keeps

To such trends as the popularity of the Pill, the sanction of premarital cohabitation, the growing approval of homosexuality, and the adoption of situation ethics, we may add another trend — the life styles that send the husband traveling around the country and frequently place the wife out in the workaday world. Both husband and wife have many opportunities to cultivate friendships with other men and women, often leading to relationships that undercut their marriage. The possible independence of both marriage partners makes marriage a good deal more loose than it was before. We have arrived at the point where marriage is no longer for keeps.

We are fast moving into an era when the only hope for a truly useful, wholesome marriage is that both husband and wife understand the Bible's view and try their level best to live in a Christian way with one another. The powers that are now able to destroy marriage are so great that the only people who will be able to establish a marriage that will hold out and help both partners will be those who know what it means to express the Christian point of view in this most intimate of human relationships.

The Bible frequently emphasizes the high value of marriage and goes so far as to urge people to become married so that they will be able to enjoy its benefits, live in purity, and contribute to the procreation of the race. Two of the well-known Ten Commandments deal with marriage, one directly when it prohibits adultery, and the other indirectly when it tells children to honor their fathers and their mothers. The Bible stresses the naturalness and wholesomeness of a man and woman leaving their parents and living together in marriage so that they become one flesh.

All this is very interesting, but the question remains: How can you be sure that you will have a marriage that will last in this age when marriages are breaking up all over and the very institution is being questioned? Here, too, the Bible is helpful. In fact, if you are serious about your marriage, you had better listen to the Bible first of all, before you listen to the latest marriage counselors.

In Ephesians 5 there is an interesting passage that is full of useful insights into the marriage relationship. The last verse sums up the Biblical formula for an enduring marriage when it says, ". . . however, let each one of you love his wife as himself, and let the wife see that she respects her husband."

It may be true, as the song says, that love and marriage go together as a horse and carriage, but love and reverence must go together once a marriage has become a fact if the marriage is going to endure. Love and reverence — the one we can understand; the other makes us throw up our hands in dismay. How many wives have you met lately who reverence their husbands? Who ever heard of anything so ridiculous? Yet our modern views of marriage have not done too much for the institution as such, so perhaps it is worth while to look at these Biblical ideas even if they seem strange to us.

Okay, you say, love I can understand, but reverence, that's something else again. But let's not be too sure we understand the love part of the sentence from the Bible that says that husbands are to love their wives and wives are to reverence their husbands. Of course, we do a great deal of talking about love nowadays. Even the great dissenters proclaim that we should make love and not make war. Love, we are told, makes the world go round. But the love people are talking about today is not a love that strengthens marriage at all.

In fact, marriage is being dissolved by love today. That seems strange, but it is true. The love men think about, when they use the word, is often very physical and very little more. We are being told that it can be expressed sexually in many different directions, even between men and men and women and women. We are also told that the long-held idea that man is a monogamous animal is just as false as false can be. He is capable of loving a number of people, if not at the same time, at least at different stages of his emotional and intellectual development. Therefore, in the name of the naturalistic view of love that is floating around, we are told that premarital sex and a few discreet extramarital sallies once in a while can actually do you good. Love, you see, as it is presently understood, is becoming the great enemy of marriage. Who would have thought that could happen?

The Bible has nothing against sexual love as this is expressed within marriage, you can be sure of that. But it is not talking about that first of all when it says in Ephesians 5:25 that husbands are to love their wives. Love, in the Bible, is the unselfish, outgoing, careful attention human beings give each other in their need. For example, you have heard of the parable of the Good Samaritan. It is a story designed to show what it means to love your neighbor. The Bible says that we are to love our neighbor as ourselves, and in the parable of the Good Samaritan it shows that loving your neighbor means helping him when he is in trouble, binding up his wounds, and setting him on the road to recovery.

At its fullest, love in the Bible has been displayed in the life, death, and resurrection of Jesus Christ. This is why, at the beginning of Ephesians 5, the chapter that says husbands are to love their wives, the Bible calls attention to the love of God revealed in Christ when it says, "Therefore be imitators of God, as beloved children. And walk in love, as Christ loved us and gave himself up for us, a fragrant offering and sacrifice to God."

The love God wants husbands to show their wives must be the highest and fullest expression of this love for the neighbor God demands of all men. For the husband, his wife is his nearest neighbor. He is in a position to know her better than he knows anyone else. He knows her hopes, her fears, and her aspirations. He knows when she is strong, and he knows when she is weak. And the Bible says that a husband is responsible for his wife's deepest welfare.

If this is necessary for an abiding marriage, it is not hard to understand why so many of them are on precarious ground. Initially, many men are attracted to their wives for the most frivolous reasons. They look on them as a sex partner and plaything, and when certain things happen so that this element in their wives diminishes, they move along to someone else.

Both husbands and wives go through a lot together and things get pretty tense sometimes. This is precisely why the kind of love the Bible says is so essential can exist and flourish only when husband and wife have attitudes that come from an understanding of the Bible's view of marriage. A man who is overwhelmed because he knows that Christ has died for him though he is an undeserving sinner will be able to make a beginning in loving his wife, even when there may be things about her that make love difficult at one time or another. But the point is, it is absolutely necessary to know Christ and His love, before a husband can display the love that insures the abiding success of marriage.

But now let's take a look at the wives. They must, according to Ephesians 5:33, respect their husbands. There is no reason, of course, to believe that the call of God to their husbands does not apply to them too — all the rules for husbands apply to wives as well. But wives, in addition to the love that is required of them, must exercise respect.

We revere heads of state. Often we are very cynical about politicians, yet when the mayor, or governor, or president, or premier, or prime minister comes around, everyone treats him with respect. Why? Because we immediately acknowledge that he has great responsibility for the welfare of thousands of people. So the wife must respect her husband because she recognizes that he has special responsibilities within the marriage and the home.

But are not men and women equal? Surely they are. The Bible recognizes that they are, too. They should be considered equal politically, so far as job opportunities are concerned, and in terms of compensation and pay. The Bible has preserved the records of valiant women, strong women, influential women, and women who exercised spiritual leadership. But when you talk about marriage, you are not talking about men as men and women as women: you are talking about them as they become husbands and wives. Marriage is a special social relationship. And if you talk about equality in marriage, you are headed for disaster.

Ephesians 5 reveals the structure of marriage when it says, "Wives, be subject to your husbands, as to the Lord. For the husband is the head of the wife as Christ is the head of the church, his body, and is himself its Savior. As the church is subject unto Christ, so let wives also be subject in everything to their husbands" (vv. 22-24).

The respect the Bible talks about, you see, is rooted in a wife's ability to see that God has appointed her husband as her spiritual guide. Just as Christ exercises loving direction over His church, so the husband is called to exercise loving direction over his wife and his family. As he does this, he may expect the respect of his wife and of his children. When you see that this respect for the husband is related to the husband's function as spiritual head of the house, it begins to make a good deal of sense.

We have departed so far from the Biblical ideal of marriage, that we can scarcely understand what it could possibly mean for a woman to exercise respect for her husband because he is the spiritual head of the house. How many women ever think of these things when they are looking for a husband? As men are often guilty of wrong attitudes when they look for a wife, women, too, often approach marriage very improperly. They think of a husband as someone who will satisfy their sexual needs, as someone who will assure them of a certain social status and provide them with a certain standard of living. None of these considerations is wrong in itself. But how many women think about their prospective husbands' spiritual qualities?

39

Will he be the kind of a person who will be able to exercise spiritual and moral leadership within the home, and will he be the kind of person a wife can look to in the years ahead for guidance and help on the deepest level of life? These, too, are important questions — the most important of all. Because they are so seldom asked, the respect the Bible talks about is seldom expressed in marriage today.

The only kind of marriage that can endure in our age of vicious attack upon the very institution of marriage itself is the marriage that is formed by the Bible's high view. A husband and wife who have never settled their basic spiritual questions and have persistently disregarded the Bible's message concerning Christ and His love for them, cannot expect to love each other properly. The marriage is bound to be built on shaky ground, and it will not take very much to send it clattering to destruction.

Once again we see how utterly important Christ is and faith in Him is. If you are already married and your marriage is in shambles, you must understand that the love and respect that is so essential if marriage is to survive can become the expression of your way of life only if you know Jesus as your Savior and you have been astonished by His love for you.

The view of marriage that prevails today will ultimately bring distress and despair to our society. But the Bible's directives will bring restoration to the lives of all husbands and wives who believe in Jesus. Marriage is for keeps. It is one of God's provisions for our deepest needs. Those who submit themselves to Christ and live out of His holy Word, the Bible, discover that this is true.

5

Freedom to Marry

The problem of interracial marriage is one of the stickiest, most emotion-bound problems men have ever faced. Everybody, it seems, wants their children to marry people who are pretty much the same color. Color, evidently, is very important. To be sure, there have been a lot of problems with interracial marriages. But it is a real question whether there have been more problems with these than with the others. Recently a middle-aged couple told me that of twenty of their friends, married about the same time they had been married, only two couples were still together. And none of these marriages had been interracial. Interracial marriages can be very difficult, but then, so can marriages be difficult when both partners possess identical coloring, come from the same kinds of families, and have gone to school together.

Tom Skinner, the Negro evangelist, has said that whom a person marries is essentially his business. And there is a lot of truth to that. The problems involved in interracial marriages should not be discounted; few will contend that such marriages are the greatest. But there is such a thing as a freedom and right to marry, just as there is a right to vote, and a right to life, liberty, and the pursuit of happiness. In fact, marriage perhaps could well come under the latter category, the pursuit of happiness. Marriage is a highly personal affair, and it is very dangerous to lay down a broad, sweeping general law and say, for example, that it's a sin for black to marry white and white to marry yellow, and yellow to marry red, and so on around the whole color wheel. Tom Skinner is right: Marriage is a personal thing, and it's not my business to interfere when two responsible people decide that they want to spend the rest of their lives together.

Whom you marry is your business. It's yours and God's. Yes, marriage is that important. God doesn't take a casual attitude regarding the marriages that are made on this earth. The Bible emphasizes again and again that ultimately the destiny of our nation, to say nothing of personal happiness or lack of it, is dependent upon how seriously people take the whole matter of courtship and marriage. It would be difficult to prove that God is as concerned about racial intermarriage as we are, but it would not be difficult to prove that He is interested in marriage. He is interested in yours, you can be sure of that.

If you are at that stage of life right now where you are beginning to think seriously about taking the step, and you are getting a little more serious about your dates and what happens on them, you can be sure that God is interested in what is going on, too. God has laid down a few rules that should govern dating patterns and the marriages that result from them. And if we could just get half as excited about the real issues of marriage as we are about such things as racial intermarriage, we would be a long way along the road to solving some of the ugly problems that fester like a cancer in our nation at this time.

In I Corinthians 7:39 God lays down one of His main principles governing marriage. First Corinthians 7 is a very interesting and even puzzling chapter. It appears at first glance to urge people not to get married at all. That's because some of the early Christians were very puzzled about whether or not they could serve God in the married state. And the apostle Paul, in I Corinthians 7, assured them that it was often advisable to remain unmarried because of the critical nature of the times in which Christians then were living. Those who were not married could serve God unencumbered by family affairs. But the general principle that emerges from this chapter is that marriage is lawful and honorable. Anyone who wants to get married should never feel that God considers the single state, or the state of virginity, essentially better than the married state. Every person should feel perfectly free to get married. It's his business, and he can choose any one he pleases — except for one thing.

And that exception is worth looking at. The Bible zeroes in on widows who were reluctant to marry for the second time. Perhaps they felt that if God had taken their first husbands away, they should feel that providentially He was preparing them for a life of single service. Or they might have been so impressed with the memory of their departed husbands that they were reluctant to marry someone else — perhaps they felt that by marrying again they would be unfaithful to their first husbands. In speaking to them, the Bible states one of the most important principles that govern marriage. This is what it says: "A wife is bound to her husband as long as he lives. If the husband dies, she is free to be married to whom she wishes, only in the Lord."

That's the principle. You are free to marry whomever you want and whoever wants you, so long as you marry in the Lord. Obviously, this principle is important for Christian people primarily. People who don't know anything about the Lord Jesus Christ and who live in rebellion against Him will have to work out their marriage problems their own way. But if you are thinking about marriage, it will be worth your while to pay attention to this Biblical principle even if you don't know the Lord yourself right now. Marriage is in desperate trouble today, and yours could well end up in disaster if you don't have something special right at the start that will guarantee its success. If you don't know the Lord, it could be the best thing in the world for you to see what the Lord can do for marriage. Maybe this is all you need to make you see that you need Jesus and you need a life's partner who is committed to Jesus right along with you.

You are free to marry, only in the Lord — that's the important qualification. Why do you need the Lord so very much in connection with marriage? Often you hear that religion is such a personal matter that you cannot insist that the person you are married to share yours with you. How many young people thinking about getting married ever think about religion? If the question comes up, the whole matter is dismissed with a flippant, "You go to your church, and I'll go to mine." Or they say, "After a few months, we'll decide what church we are going to attend." But as a matter of fact, once they get married neither of them gives the matter of his faith much attention and often neither of them goes to church, and their children are reared with no faith to guide them.

If you are thinking about getting married, the question of whether you and your life's partner are one in the Lord Jesus Christ is the most important single question you face. Whether or not your fiance loves the Lord Jesus Christ and wants to serve Him is a lot more important than whether or not she wears clothes well and a bathing suit better. Whether or not your boy friend knows Jesus is more important than whether or not he is still taller than you are when you wear high heels. Often, when people think of marriage today, they think about a whole host of essentially foolish, frivolous matters that aren't going to make one bit of difference twenty years from now if they are still together. The most important thing in all the world is whether or not both you and your marriage partner know the Lord and want to serve Him.

Why is this? Why is it so utterly necessary to marry "in the Lord"? It is so important because marriage is such an intensely intricate and delicate human relationship that it is subject to immense and shattering pressures. The Bible says that God created man in His own image, ". . . male and female created He them" (Genesis 1:27). And we are told, further, that for this reason a man shall leave his father and his mother and be joined to his wife and the two are to become one (Matthew 19:5). All this shows that marriage is one of the most important aspects of human life. Within the bonds of holy matrimony men and women are given the opportunity to share a unity of ideas, aspirations, and interests that is so intimate that they are virtually one flesh. All this is sealed, confirmed, and sustained by the mysterious sexual union that flourishes at the center of all good marriages.

Because of the intricacy and the delicacy of the marriage relationship, marriage is dynamite. A good marriage can help two people grow far beyond the point either of them would have attained alone. But a bad one is a miserable, debilitating, crippling experience that drives people up the walls in frustration.

There is every evidence to support the conclusion

that the demonic forces that are abroad in this world are especially focused on turning marriages into pitfalls of misery and temptation. Because marriage is so complex, it can be tipped off balance very easily.

Look at all the things that can put a backbreaking strain on a marriage. We marry for better or worse, don't forget. And often when things get better, marriage gets worse. Husbands who have suddenly achieved success and financial affluence have often left their poor wives wishing for the simpler days when their hubby was around the house a couple evenings of the week. Husbands and wives must go through a lot together. You generally get married when you are young and strong and as handsome or beautiful as you will ever be. But when illness strikes and you have to grab hold of each other's arms and help each other walk along and nurse one another back to health — that's a different matter.

In addition to all this, there are the internal strains of the home and the family. Children can cause problems. There is money with all the "fun" it brings trying to figure out how to spend it properly and manage to save a little for your children's college education. Once you say, "I do," you are in for twenty-four hours of every day from then on working things out together and trying to make your lives together useful and joy-filled.

This is why Christ is so necessary. A young couple who both want to serve Jesus will find that there are broad areas of their lives about which they entirely agree. And they are important areas. They will see eye to eye on many subjects which are essentially religious matters. There are all kinds of ethical questions connected with marriage: How large should your family be? Should you buy a new davenport or give more money to charity? What kind of an education should your children be given? And what about drink in the home, and other kinds of conduct? Are you going to agree on these matters, or will they be a source of constant fighting and bickering?

The point is this: If two people are not agreed on the basic religious matters of life, they don't have much chance in marriage. When they are both agreed and both serving Jesus, there are still going to be large areas of conflict and tension. But serving Christ together brings to a marriage a plus factor that can never be valued enough.

But there is one other thing that makes it so important to marry in the Lord. Two people who both know the Lord Jesus Christ, and want to live their lives in His kingdom, know a secret formula that takes our ordinary humdrum lives and turns them into something fine. What is that secret? It is the secret of forgiveness.

The Bible says, you are free to marry, only be sure you marry in the Lord. What does it mean to be in the Lord? It means to be astonished by the matchless love of the living God who has expressed His love by sending His only begotten Son into the world to take away the sins of all who believe on Him. In Jesus, God comes to men with the offer of forgiveness. And when they believe in this Jesus, that forgiveness becomes their possession. They know that the great God of heaven and earth has taken all their sins away and now they are really free to live joy-filled, important lives themselves.

Those who are still single and are thinking about getting married cannot begin to know how delicate marriage really is until after they have been married. Because marriage is the kind of intimate relationship it is, a relationship in which the husband and wife get to know each other very well after a while, there are hundreds of situations that come up every week that can make a husband and wife hate each other. Yes, it can get that bad after a while.

Husbands and wives sometimes offend each other; they hurt each other, they are rude to each other, and they become angry with each other. And when these things happen, somewhere along the line there must be forgiveness. All the stresses and strains of marriage cannot be overcome by a large dose of romantic love, whatever that is. Marriage must be graced by the redeeming virtue of forgiveness.

When you know that your marriage partner is a forgiven sinner and you know that Christ has forgiven you, too, in spite of all your sins, you can forgive one another. But those who do not know the Lord will often find their hatreds, disappointments, and deep running resentments growing and growing through the years, so that finally both of them retire into their own private corners and each goes his own way. They are left with the husk of what used to be a beautiful life of love.

Today young people are getting married for all kinds of reasons, and many of the reasons are bad. They stream through the marriage mills and through the municipal courts on Saturday morning, couple after couple after couple. Some get married in the solemnity of a church. But a pathetic number of the marriages have nothing to do with God and the Lord Jesus Christ. The couple getting married does not know about Jesus and does not care about Him.

Don't let that happen to you. Be sure that you know the Lord Jesus as your Savior yourself and then pray and pray until God sends you someone who knows Jesus the same way you do. If you marry in the Lord your friends can commit you both to the Lord Jesus Christ. They will be able to pray this way about you:

O perfect Love, all human thought transcending,
Lowly we kneel in prayer before Thy throne,
That theirs may be the love which knows no ending,
Whom Thou in sacred vow dost join in one.

O perfect Life, be Thou their full assurance,
Of tender charity and stedfast faith,
Of patient hope and quiet, brave endurance,
With childlike trust that fears no pain nor death.

Grant them the joy which brightens earthly sorrow;
Grant them the peace which calms all earthly strife,
And to life's day the glorious unknown morrow
That dawns upon eternal love and life.

Those who marry in the Lord can live their lives surrounded by the love of Jesus. And marriage is too important to enter any other way.

6

Incompatibility in Marriage

If you are married or you are going to get married, you might as well expect that you and your mate will be incompatible. You know what that means, don't you? It means that each of you will have characteristics that irritate the other insufferably. And it means that there will be certain types of circumstances in which each of you consistently brings out the worst in the other. Sometimes it is sexual incompatibility that is the villain, sometimes it is emotional incompatibility, sometimes it is financial incompatibility, sometimes it is temperamental — but whatever it is, it is extremely unpleasant, and the chances of there being some of it in your marriage run about 90 percent, perhaps even 99 percent.

That there is a certain amount of incompatibility in every marriage is the basic assumption Cecil G. Osborne makes in his book, *The Art of Understanding Your Mate*. Mr. Osborne's frank recognition of incompatibility is certainly supported by the facts today. Incompatibility of various kinds is contributing to the general collapse of marriage as an institution. The situation has deteriorated so much recently that Herbert A. Otto, a Fellow of the American Association of Marriage Counselors, has recently raised the question, "Has Monogamy Failed?" Well, whether or not it has failed, one thing is certain, it is hardly in style anymore, and apparently few people really want to give

50

it a good lifetime try. A cartoon appeared recently that showed a bride looking at her groom with a toothy smile and declaring, "Darling! Our first marriage." This is a rather accurate description of the present state of affairs. Those who know the profile of the latest divorce statistics are saying that we are close to the day when 85 percent of all men and women reaching the age of sixty-five will have been remarried at least once. So, the gushing remark of the new bride about their "first marriage" was very appropriate.

If a married couple are incompatible it means very simply that the two do not always "get along very well." There is nothing new about this. Adam and Eve didn't see eye to eye on everything, Abraham and Sarah disagreed occasionally, and Isaac and Rebekah had their quarrels. But today incompatibility is contributing to the breakup of marriage as never before because of new attitudes. If people find that they are at odds with their mate they are just not going to put up with it anymore. In his article that questions the strength of monogamy, Herbert Otto documents the casual approach people have to divorce today, and he shows how society is prepared for more and more divorce. This is what he says:

"The other day a good friend, senior executive of a large company and in his early forties, dropped by for a visit. He told me he had been thinking of divorce after sixteen years of marriage. The couple have a boy, twelve, and two girls, one of whom is ten, the other eight. My friend said, 'We've grown apart over the years, and we have nothing in common left anymore other than the children. There are at least twenty years of enjoying life still ahead of me. I was worried about the children until we discussed it with them. So many of their schoolmates had had divorced parents or

51

parents who had remarried, they are accustomed to the idea. It's part of life. Of course, if the older ones need help, I want them to see a good psychiatrist while we go through with this. My wife is still a good-looking woman, younger than I, and probably will remarry. I'm not thinking of it now, but I'll probably remarry someday.' " Mr. Otto concludes by saying, "This situation illustrates an attitude and the climate of the times. Divorce has become as much an institution as marriage."

Not everyone is as well off financially as this fine senior executive was and so not everyone can contemplate divorce with such calm detachment. But the fact remains that divorce is a part of the times in which we live and because it is, incompatibility is more disastrous now than ever before. This means that if you are concerned about the future of your marriage, you should begin right now to take steps to preserve it, before it is too late. Regardless of what men are saying today, your future happiness depends on the strength and usefulness of your marriage. Divorce is crippling for the people involved and it is frequently disastrous for the children, in spite of the fact that divorced parents are now sometimes considerate enough to send the children to a psychiatrist while the ugly proceedings are taking place. Children of divorced parents get divorces themselves, more often than not. And so the ugly downward spiral continues until the whole nation will finally be filled with homeless children and with marriages that are due to collapse any minute.

The damaging results of broken marriages should not be surprising when we consider the basic fact that God Almighty has made marriage holy and guarded it with His own great law. One of the Ten Commandments says, "You shall not commit adultery," and this implies that everyone of us is obligated to God to work hard at the preservation of his marriage. Marriage is holy, yours is, or yours will be when finally you are married, and because it is, you must work hard at yours. If you don't you are going to be in trouble with God and you will reap the bitter fruit that disobedience always brings. That sounds strange — to say that those who allow their marriage to disintegrate will be in trouble with God. It sounds strange because this world has departed so very far from God. But the fact that many people have departed from God does not alter the facts. And the fact is, the Bible requires husbands and wives to consider their marriages sacred and they must see to it that theirs endures, until death finally breaks it.

The point is that the only way you are going to be able to make a go of your marriage is that you begin by taking the Bible's point of view concerning marriage very seriously. This does not mean just avoiding divorce. This means making your marriage as great and wonderful as God intended it to be. After all, it is not enough to avoid divorce. Marriage, if it is to bestow the greatest benefits upon both partners and upon the children born of the marriage relationship, should be joy filled, and sustaining. Those who begin theirs in the light of the Bible have a good chance of having that kind of a marriage.

You would be surprised how much the Bible has to say about marriage. In addition to the commandment prohibiting adultery, the Bible has many words of advice for husbands and wives. One of them is found in the First Letter of Peter in the New Testament, the third chapter. Verse 7 says, ". . . husbands, live considerately with your wives, bestowing honor on the

53

woman as the weaker sex, since you are joint heirs of the grace of life, in order that your prayers may not be hindered."

The apostle Peter is able to give us some very good advice about this subject, because he was himself a married man and he knew what he was talking about. He tells us some very important things about marriage that are worth paying attention to. This is what they are:

First of all, the Bible recognizes that there are always going to be incompatibilities in marriage. The Bible comes out flatfooted and declares that women are the weaker sex. Now that must give Betty Friedan and all the others in the women's liberation movement apoplexy, but that is what the Bible says.

Those who have not been carried away by the rhetoric of the women's liberation movement and other similar movements throughout the years admit that this is really so — women *are* the weaker sex. You can attribute this statement to male stupidity and arrogance if you wish, and you can point out that women live longer and what not, but by and large, in general, from a worldwide point of view, from a world historical perspective, what the Bible says is true. Whatever you want to say about the role of women in business, or in sports, or in entertainment, or even in religious life, there can be no doubt that the Bible considers them the weaker sex in the home and the family. If you are honest, whether you are a man or a woman, you will have to agree that this is a rather accurate description. There are many homes that are held together by the indomitable, courageous spirit of a wife who has a weak, good-for-nothing husband. This is true. But the Bible still insists that within the framework of the home and the family we should begin by recognizing that women are the weaker sex.

The Bible does not perpetuate this idea, which may be offensive to some, in order to downgrade women and keep them in their place, but in order to highlight this far more important fact: the greatest responsibility for the stability and health of the marriage lies with the men. The man is the head of the house. Old fashioned? Perhaps, but it is a sound principle, and one of the reasons the home is in such shambles today is that so many people are discarding this Biblical principle.

This means, practically, that you husbands must understand that the responsibility for the health of your marriage is yours first of all. So don't go running off to some marriage counselor with complaints about your wife until you have done your best to help your wife overcome some of her difficulties. Surely she has problems; you should expect that. But you are responsible to stand by her and help her meet them and solve them. One of the big troubles today is that most people think of marriage as a two-way street, a fifty-fifty proposition and once the wife doesn't measure up, the husband figures he has every right in the world to discard her. The Bible says, "No, Mr. Smith. You are responsible for your wife's welfare. Start with that."

The Bible is very down to earth about this. It says "Husbands, live considerately with your wives. . . ." A good many marriages would be saved if husbands would begin with this simple matter, being considerate of their wives. The simple fact is that thousands of marriages today are breaking up because the husbands are so selfish and spoiled they think only of themselves and their welfare. They are more considerate of the people at work than they are of their wives. The healing of broken marriages has to begin somewhere, and

55

a good place to start is where the Bible starts, with husbands recognizing their special responsibility. Once they do, we can expect the wives to live up to theirs, too.

Perhaps this point irks you. The Bible does not emphasize this to rub salt into old wounds. It calls husbands to live considerately with their wives in order that together they may express their common faith in the Lord Jesus Christ. Once a man's marriage has gone sour, just about everything else in his life is going to go sour, too. There is no way to avoid that. And Peter says that husbands should live considerately with their wives because they are both joint heirs of the grace of life, and they must overcome their incompatibilities so that their "prayers will not be hindered," as he puts it.

What the Bible is saying here is that the husbands must be considerate of their wives, not because their wives are *weaker,* but because they, with their wives, are both equal in God's sight. The Bible does not say that women are inferior to men, so far as God is concerned. It says quite the opposite. It says, for example, that in Christ the distinction between male and female is inconsequential. Galatians 3 says this: "For as many of you as were baptized into Christ have put on Christ. There is neither Jew nor Greek, there is neither slave nor free, there is neither male nor female; for you are all one in Christ Jesus" (vv. 27, 28). According to the Bible, a husband and wife can stand together before Jesus Christ as equal, as people who together have received the grace of Christ and the power of the Holy Spirit. Therefore Peter says to husbands, "Live considerately with your wife — because you are both one in the Lord." Your wife is not just a servant or a sexual plaything that exists to take care of your children and be around when you happen to want her. But you, with her, are both children of God who have been saved by Jesus' blood.

Right here we get down to the main thing that is going to make a marriage work by enabling both marriage partners to overcome their incompatibilities and live together in a God honoring way. When Peter wrote this, he knew that a healthy marriage depended upon both husband and wife believing on the Lord Jesus Christ. That was true then. It is just as true today, when naturalistic, selfish views of marriage prevail and conduct in marriage has deteriorated to an all time low.

If you are Christian people living together as husband and wife, but your marriage is on the skids and your incompatibilities are driving you both up the wall, maybe you just haven't looked at one another as fellow Christians should. What about it, Mr. Smith, do you think of your wife as a sister in the Lord? Maybe you had better start doing that, if she is, in fact, such a sister. And then you should be considerate of her needs. A husband who looks at his wife that way is going to be able to help her be a better wife and mother.

There is no use beating around the bush about this matter of incompatibility. Unless your marriage is a marriage in which both you and your wife (or husband) are people who believe in the Lord Jesus Christ, whatever you do to overcome the incompatibilities you have will fall short of success. This doesn't mean that once two people believe in the Lord as their Savior everything will be fine for them. Anyone who knows anything about the present state of Christian marriages knows that Christians have all kinds of problems in their marriages, too. But, because of their common faith, they are often able to work out their difficulties together.

The apostle Peter concludes his word with the husbands by saying that they are to live considerately with their wives in order that their prayers may not be hindered. This is where the marriage of two people who both believe receives its healing and the strength to advance — at the place of prayer. A husband and wife who recognize each other as children of God who have been saved by the cross of Jesus Christ are able to pray together. They can pray for one another. They can pray when their incompatibilities seem more than either of them can bear. They can pray when sickness comes and financial crises make the foundation of their marriage shudder. They can pray together for their children. They can pray for others. And as they do, they will find that their marriage will become the sacred holy thing God intended it to be, a source of strength and blessing that will enable both of them to be better people.

There will be incompatibilities in every marriage. There is no escaping that. There will be in yours as well. And today when people are discarding marriage for any reason whatever, you may be sure that unless you find a way to cope with the incompatibilities in yours, your marriage will not last very long. Or even if it does, it will not be very satisfactory.

If you want a marriage that is good and will endure, look to Jesus. When a husband and wife kneel at His cross together they will both be healed. If you are not married yet, be sure you get a mate who can kneel with you there. And if you are married, why don't you and your mate kneel and ask Christ to be your Savior and the Savior of your marriage right now, or at least some time before this long dark day is over?

7

In Defense of Motherhood

In spite of the fact that the second Sunday in May is set aside as Mother's Day, motherhood as such is declining in popularity. Mother's Day is celebrated in one way or another in many countries and it has even been officially recognized by the Congress of the United States. But declining birth rates and shrinking family size in many parts of the world suggest that people actually think of motherhood in terms other than those their celebration of Mother's Day would suggest.

Millions of mothers receive honor from their children while they themselves dishonor motherhood. They dishonor it by carefully restricting their family size because of their own selfish interests. Though there are no medical reasons or other equally important reasons for limiting their families, they carefully keep their families small and manageable. In the United States alone, millions of women take birth control pills each month.

It would be a mistake to assume that those who are restricting their family size to one or two children are doing so because of a desire to do their part in solving the problem of the population explosion. The problem of population explosion, particularly as it occurs in poverty stricken, underdeveloped nations, will certainly not be solved by the practice of birth control on the part of people who are relatively rich and entirely capable of feeding, clothing, and educating their offspring. Those who practice birth control measures for selfish reasons are not trying to solve the parking problem in our large cities, as some bumper stickers facetiously suggest. In most cases they are doing so because they consider motherhood a bore and a burden. A good many women, with the full support of their husbands, do not wish to be involved in it except at their own convenience. And they define their convenience very narrowly.

It is very difficult to find someone who is saying something positive about motherhood today. The prevailing attitudes respecting this institution are generally negative. One mother, who happens to be the wife of a clergyman, expresses the modern point of view very well when she says, "Motherhood has an amazing capacity to tear up, splinter our personhood, show up our shortcomings." This is a matter not of devotion or lack of devotion but of hard fact. A more realistic word to mothers would seem to be: "Hold on, this too will pass away; in the meantime refresh yourself with some life of your own, apart from your children."

Many would agree with this statement. Therefore many young people who get married today have no intention of having children for a good long time. Those who do have children often try to escape the responsibilities of motherhood as soon as possible. Betty Friedan, in her book, *The Feminine Mystique,* explicitly states that motherhood and the home does not present the modern well-educated housewife with an adequate challenge. It is not at all strange that today four of every ten mothers who have children of school age are working outside the home. Obviously, not all of them are forced to do so because of financial problems. The flight from the home is often prompted by a growing consensus that the home is a frustrating drag and is not worthy of a woman's emotional power and creative talent.

There is no question about it: the care of the children is a task that is often exceedingly difficult and heartbreaking. Nevertheless, a careless, easy avoiding of this task through the use of birth control measures will ultimately cause more difficulties than it will remove. If birth control is practiced because of the wife's, and husband's, improper view of motherhood itself, very serious emotional and spiritual problems will occur. The question of family size is ultimately an ethical question of the highest order. It is a spiritual issue in which every mother, and father too, is confronted with the soul searching question: what is the will of God for my life? This question can be answered only in the light of the Bible's data concerning children and their importance.

The Christian Reformed Church has a very useful statement on birth control that should be helpful for all those who are faced with this question today. It was written some years ago, at the depths of the Depression, as a matter of fact. Thus, it has not been prejudiced by some of the elements that are a part of the current discussion of this subject. It speaks to the current situation with a unique freshness. The fact that it was written more than thirty years ago is a tribute to those who at that time were already concerned to discover how the Bible viewed birth control practices.

The *Testimony on Birth Control of the Christian Reformed Church* is distinguished by a broad view of marriage and its meaning. Referring to the information in Genesis about the institution of marriage, the *Testimony* indicates that marriage is for both the physical and emotional well-being of the marriage partners,

61

and also for the procreation of children. Both of these aspects of marriage are treated as equally important. With respect to family size, the *Testimony* suggests that it should be "compatible with the mental and spiritual wellbeing of the wife and mother on the one hand, and of the children on the other."

The *Testimony* concludes with this final statement: "[The final decision regarding family size] is, in the last analysis, a distinctly personal matter, which husband and wife must settle in the presence of their God and in the light of the best medical advice. . . . Living as we do in a world suffering from the ravages of sin, certain conditions and circumstances may demand of Christians that they forego parenthood, or that the voluntary limiting of the number of their offspring becomes their duty before God. While making full allowance for this personal and medical angle of the matter, . . . it is the solemn duty of the church to bear testimony against the growing evil of selfish birth restriction and to hold up the sacred ordinances of God and the Christian ideal of marriage and parenthood, which are increasingly being ignored and flouted in our day. Childbearing and parenthood are to be held up as a basic aim of marriage. The glory of fatherhood and motherhood, which Scripture stresses so repeatedly, should be made real upon proper occasion in the preaching and teaching of the church, and especially in the thought, the conversation, and the life of all those who name themselves after Christ."

Notice this statement does not say that limitation of family size is necessarily evil in itself. But it does call attention to a "selfish restriction of family size" that is evil. Isn't it true that a "selfish restriction of family size" is very prevalent today? Because of the availability of birth control pills and devices, many couples simply assume that they can do as they please with respect to this matter. Their decision is purely naturalistic. They consider only their own wants and desires, their own goals and dreams. They feel that the size of their family is their own business. It *is* their business, but it is *God's* business too. If their final decision is going to be beneficial for them, for society, and for the church, it will have to take into consideration the will of God for their lives.

In the final analysis, no clergyman nor church today, can lay down specific guidelines that will remove the responsibility for final decision from the couple directly involved. The *Testimony on Birth Control of the Christian Reformed Church* emphasizes this point. But the church would be seriously remiss in its duty if it failed to insist that every married couple make their decision in the light of the Bible's statements concerning marriage, parenthood, and children.

What is the Bible's message concerning children? It is very simply this: Children are God's great gift. Perhaps we could go so far as to say that they are His greatest natural gift to His people. The Biblical point of view is found in a verse like Psalm 127:3. Here we read, "Lo, sons are a heritage from the Lord, the fruit of the womb a reward." Children are God's reward. Children? With all their problems, their sickness, their stubbornness, the grief they bring — these are God's reward? What about parents who have retarded children or crippled children? A young mother might smile at the irony of it and say, "My children are God's reward? My children who keep me awake at night, who are there first thing in the morning with their demands and who keep me a slave, a prisoner, in my home all day long — these are God's reward?"

This is what the Bible says, and it is often true that

the revelation of God seems to contradict our own experience. But there you have it, and this revelation provides Christian mothers, Christian parents, with the strength to receive their children with thankfulness and raise them with patience and love. Children and the discipline they carry into our lives, the problems they force us to face and solve, everything about them is somehow God's way of rewarding His people. When children are received with this knowledge and understanding, He provides grace to those whom He has called to parenthood, and God makes their experiences with their children the most meaningful, satisfying, and spiritually helpful experiences they ever have.

The Bible continually promotes a view of motherhood that is beautiful and exalted. The very physical aspects of motherhood, today so often despised and joked about, are the object of awesome wonder in the Bible. Ecclesiastes 11:5 says, "As you do not know how the spirit comes to the bones in the womb of a woman with child, so you do not know the work of God who makes everything." The mystery of the formation of a person within a mother's womb stands as the mystery that puts to rest all human arrogance and pretense. The Bible speaks with delicacy and wonder as it describes the precious and intimate relationship that exists between a mother and her infant.

Furthermore the Bible provides us with many examples of mothers who exercised decisive influence in the lives of their children. Moses, the great leader of the people of Israel, though adopted in a pagan household, did not leave the influence of his mother until she had taught him the fundamental doctrines of the Hebrew religion, doctrines that never left him and made it possible for him to become the great leader of the people of God. It was Jacob's mother who helped burn into his soul a passionate love for the promises of God so that he was willing to move heaven and earth to acquire the blessings of the covenant. The tender story of Hannah, the mother who prayed for a son from God, is well-known to many children in Sunday school. Her prayers were answered when she was given Samuel who became a great prophet and judge.

Even Jesus Christ appears in the Bible as the Son of the Virgin Mary, according to the flesh. That the Son of God would have a mother is almost impossible to imagine, but it is true. We meet her frequently on the pages of the Gospels, often in the background, but often there, somehow contributing to the events of Jesus' life. When the sword finally tore her son's body, she felt it in her own bones, because she saw it happen on Calvary. The evidence for the high glory of motherhood is overwhelming in the Bible. When God bestows upon a woman in the marriage state the gift of motherhood, He honors her and calls her to a high vocation.

Motherhood provides a woman with a challenge of the highest order, one that will tax all her wisdom, utilize all her emotional qualities, and often put to work whatever other skills she may possess. Mothers are given the priceless opportunity of dealing with the well-springs of human life. It is from their mothers that children acquire their basic attitudes and points of view. It is their mother who molds them and directs them. Ultimately a mother holds within her hands the very destiny of the world. There is nothing wrong, of course, in mothers working outside the home under certain circumstances — it may be good for them. But it is ridiculous to suggest that this is necessary because a mother's work within the home is meaningless and dull. Isn't it true that many women flee their homes because the high calling of motherhood is just too much for them? It demands resources which they simply do not have. And they do not have the resources necessary because they have never looked at their tasks in the light of the Bible and asked God for the wisdom and the strength and the victory He alone can give.

Don't you think that one of the basic reasons marriages and families are the scene of so many problems is this: a great many married women have never faced their real responsibilities with respect to motherhood? Consequently they resent their children, and they also resent their husbands. Why is it that so many of those marriages in which the husband and wife have decided to wait four, five, or more years before the first baby are marriages that have become desperately unhappy in spite of the fact that they have plenty of money, a sporty new car, and a good start on the down payment on their new house? Why is it that there are so many unhappy families — families in which the parents have very prudently limited their offspring so that there is plenty for everyone? Could one of the reasons be that people who limit their families for selfish reasons despise one of God's greatest gifts and choose instead the gifts that men can give them? A new car, a new home — these are not really gifts of God in the fullest sense. But a baby is. Every baby is born because of God's miracle, and when a father and mother receive their children, they receive them from His hand. "Lo, sons are a heritage from the Lord, the fruit of the womb a reward."

Children are God's great gift to His people. No advance of medical science may ever blind us to this essential fact. Motherhood is one of the highest honors God confers upon women. Those who, for selfish reasons, refuse to receive God's gift of children run the risk of receiving His judgment in their place.

8

Planning for Parenthood

The Canadian nation has long been known for its exceptional interest in the families that comprise it. Madame Vanier, the distinguished wife of the late governor general, has typified this interest. The Vanier Institute of the Family, named in her honor, provides the nation with useful insights into family problems. Recognizing that some might be deterred from having families because of financial considerations, the government has made special provision for children's welfare — Canadian citizens receive a children's allowance from the government. Obviously Canada knows that the health of the nation is dependent upon the well-being of the family.

Family size, of course, is just one aspect of family life within a nation. Quantity is one thing, but quality is even more important. In its centennial year, Canada pointed the way to the recognition of this fact too. In Saskatoon, Saskatchewan, one of the main centennial projects was a counseling course for engaged and newly married couples. Saskatoon is to be congratulated for the insights that led to the establishment of this kind of project. In the long run, the strength of a nation's families is going to be determined by the quality of family life that marks them. And that is dependent upon the moral qualities the parents possess.

In the final analysis, the characteristics of family

life are dependent upon the parents' faith in God. Doubtlessly many high government officials would admit that children's allowances and even community-wide counseling programs are going to fail if there is no deep religious faith among the parents of our land. Today we hear a great deal about planned parenthood. We associate the term often with birth control. Perhaps we should begin to speak of planned parenthood in a much broader way. There should be planning *for* parenthood. A nation should make provisions that will enable its citizens to prepare themselves for the great responsibilities of parenthood. Certainly one of the major elements in planning for parenthood is making provision for a religious situation in which parenthood can develop its most useful aspects. The Gospel of the Lord Jesus Christ has a most significant contribution to make to the health of the family. This contribution must be exploited to the full.

The Old Testament contains a record of God's gracious dealings with the Jewish people, and it points forward to the coming of Christ which is described in the New Testament. Certainly, then, the concluding words of the Old Testament, the last word of prophecy spoken before four centuries of prophetic silence, would be exceptionally significant words — and indeed they are. Amazingly they have something to say about the family: "Behold, I will send you Elijah the prophet before the great and terrible day of the Lord comes. And he will turn the hearts of the fathers to their children and the hearts of the children to their fathers, lest I come and smite the land with a curse" (Malachi 4:5-6).

This is a very obscure sounding text and it would demand many hours of study and discussion to explain it fully. Without discussing specifically the meaning of the coming of Elijah or the meaning of the great day of the Lord, one salient point cannot go unnoticed in these words that conclude the entire Old Testament portion of the Bible. These words, forming as they do a bridge between the Old Testament and the New, are a declaration that God's great work of grace, as revealed in the Old Testament and in the New, is a work of grace that brings healing into families. The prophet Malachi is saying in effect, "There's a great day coming in which the fullness of God's revelation is going to burst upon our consciousness, and then the hearts of the fathers will be turned to their children, and the hearts of the children shall be turned to the fathers." God's revelation of grace can bring fathers and children back together.

These words reflect a situation that is similar to ours today. The people of Israel were experiencing a radical breakdown in their society. After their exile, religious apostasy and moral laxity once again began to mark their lives. Few were interested in God's law and the message of the prophets. Social sins, such as divorce, were common. Then too there was a massive estrangement between the generations. The children were not interested in the message of their fathers. They were interested neither in the message of their ancient fathers who had given them the word of prophecy and the law, nor in the message of their immediate fathers who represented the authority of God in their lives. Grave disintegrating forces broke the nation, and each passing year brought the moment of crisis closer.

The breakdown between the generations that existed then has been duplicated time and time again throughout the centuries and is one of the most disturbing aspects of our own experience today. Newspapers and television accounts provide us with ongoing documentation of the collapse of social structures which two or three decades ago were considered invulnerable. The "now" generation, the "go" generation, is making it inescapably clear that it wants nothing to do with that which it considers to be the worn-out values of the past. Many parts of our modern world live in a constant state of suspended shock while teen-agers and college and university students declare that they have discarded some of the most sacred aspects of Christian culture.

But don't make the mistake of thinking that those who are discarding the norms of the past are now living lives of uninterrupted pleasure. The shock that is experienced by those who feel rejected by the younger generation finds its counterpart in the bitterness and the cynicism that marks those who should be enjoying the new freedom. The breakdown in communication between the generations has not resulted in creative tensions that hold promise for a glorious tomorrow. Instead, the shock, dismay, cynicism, and bitterness that now dominates so much of our lives renders individuals incapable of responding usefully to the great opportunities that are a part of this age.

But of course, the massive breakdown in communication between the fathers and their children, and children and their fathers, comes to its most painful expression right within our own families. It is expressed in glowering looks and the depressing silence that often cannot be broken when fathers are with their children. As children show that they are not interested in their parents' opinion and parents try unsuccessfully to make contact with the children whom they love, the deep hurt grows day after day. Finally the love that should bind the family together is replaced by suspicion and daily heartbreak.

Thus the family, the heart of the nation, becomes a field of battle. As the family disintegrates, the nation is destroyed. It is destroyed as effectively as it would be if an enemy showered it with nuclear destruction.

To all nations the last verse of the Old Testament proclaims that the revelation contained in the Bible has a solution to offer to the estrangement that now exists between the generations. How can that be? It's like this: Jesus Christ, who is the person revealed in the Bible, is uniquely qualified to bring people together. The Gospel's message is so remarkable because it appeals to people of all ages. There is no kind of person who by virtue of his place in life cannot be conquered by Christ.

Every missionary will testify that this is so. Those who have believed in the great message of redemption that has been accomplished through Christ's work on Calvary's cross feel that they are united with one another. In the Book of Acts, the second chapter, we find the record of the earliest church fellowship. That fellowship had received the gift of the Holy Spirit and the faith of every individual was intense. The Bible reveals that the members of that living church were united together. And there were all kinds of people in that church — rich and poor, and fathers and mothers with their children — with their teen-agers, as a matter of fact. But they were one, in Christ.

This is the great possibility God extends to families in His gracious revelation: the possibility of unity through a common faith in the Lord Jesus Christ. No rational person can deny that there are serious factors that impede communication between parents and their children. The experience of those who are in high school and college right now is utterly different from the experience of those who are over thirty. There is no use denying this. It is a fact. This is the reason why it is so difficult for many of us to talk together. But when people who are separated by different experiences discover that they have a common faith in Jesus Christ, the Lord of all, they discover that they are united when it comes to matters of life and death.

To be perfectly frank, there is no human way to bridge the chasm that separates the generations today. The world is moving too fast. The only way that a parent can expect to maintain vital communication with his children is this: Parents and their children must become brothers and sisters in the Lord. When they together confess a common faith in the Lord Jesus Christ, they will discover that their experiences together can be meaningful and useful in spite of the differences that exist between them.

How many people realize this today? Often Christian faith is considered a purely individual concern. There are many Christian parents who evidently feel that their own faith cannot be expected to have an effect upon their children. They look upon their children as unconverted individuals who have not yet received the Holy Spirit. They fail to see that God has proclaimed that His great revelation is designed to bring parents and their children together within a bond of fellowship that transcends natural, blood relationships. Again and again the Bible emphasizes the significance of God's grace for the family. On Pentecost day, the apostle Peter declared, "For the promise is to you *and to your children . . ."* (Acts 2:39). Paul announced to the Philippian jailer, "Believe in the Lord Jesus Christ, and you will be saved, *you and your household"* (Acts 16:31). All this indicates, at the very least, that the Christian faith has the greatest kind of contribution to make to family life. It is folly to suggest that a nation's families can be strong so long as the meaning of Christianity for the family goes unrecognized.

So then, it is absolutely necessary that a nation, in charting its future course, makes ample provision for the existence of truly Christian homes within its borders. Of course, no government may use its power to force religion upon anyone. Matters of faith are too personal for that. But there must be every opportunity given those who delight in drawing on the resources of the Christian Gospel within their homes.

Those citizens who claim to be Christians have the greatest responsibility of all. They must recognize that their tasks as parents are among the most serious of their lives and they must plan for parenthood so that they will be able to express within their families the significance of God's grace. Far too many people who claim that Jesus Christ has captured their souls, still view marriage and the family in a very naturalistic way. Young women who claim to be Christian often consent to marry someone who is not equipped to help them establish a Christian home. And Christian young men are often shockingly reckless when it comes to selecting a wife who shall ultimately make their homes what they are going to be. Planning for parenthood must include a careful preparation for the spiritual life of the home.

And those of you who are now involved in parenthood, or are looking forward to parenthood, but who do not really know the Lord Jesus Christ, I hope you understand that your home is going to be less than ideal if you do not have Christ at its center. I know that Christians too have their problems. Because the family is so complex and marvelous, there are all kinds of things that can go wrong within it. But the question is this: When things go wrong, what resources will you have to cope with the difficulties? Will you have a Savior then? And will your children have a Savior then?

The Gospel of the Lord Jesus Christ is so powerful it can unite husbands and wives, brothers and sisters, and parents and children. In this age in which society seems to be disintegrating, we need this Gospel right at the center of our nation's life — we need this Gospel within our homes.

No nation is more blessed than that nation whose homes are united around Jesus Christ. As one of the Psalms in the Old Testament puts it so very beautifully:

> O happy land, whose sons in youth,
> In sturdy strength and noble truth,
> Like plants in vigor spring;
> Whose daughters fair, a queenly race,
> Are like the cornerstones that grace
> The palace of a king.
>
> O happy land, when flock and field
> Their rich, abundant increase yield,
> And blessings multiply;
> When plenty all thy people share,
> And no invading foe is there,
> And no distressful cry.
>
> O happy people, favored land,
> To whom the Lord with liberal hand
> Has thus His goodness shown;
> Yea, surely is that people blest
> By whom Jehovah is confessed
> To be their God alone.

9

Abortion

As a part of the changing moral climate we live in, new possibilities for abortion are now available. A discussion of the present attitudes toward abortion and laws pertaining to it has stated: "In France . . . it is currently estimated by the U.N. population branch that the number of abortions greatly exceeds the annual number of registered births. Abortion has been legalized by the governments of Japan, the USSR, Communist China, some East European nations, and in Great Britain. Moreover, the Scandinavian nations are extremely permissive toward abortion." Currently in the U.S., legislators in several states have been pressured into liberalizing abortion laws. In some cases convenience and preference of the mother, rather than her life and health, are now the deciding factors.

Professor K. H. Mehlan, of East Germany, reported at a meeting of the International Federation of Gynecologists and Obstetricians that the abortion rate is like an epidemic. In his report, the East German professor highlighted the problem in Latin America where 50 percent of the pregnancies were terminated by illegal abortions.

The world-wide swing to a very liberal attitude toward abortion reflects a growing consensus that abortion laws must be modified to allow for it, not only to save the life of the mother, but also to further her social

75

well-being. In addition, there is a growing demand that abortion be employed to terminate pregnancies caused by rape and incest, and where there is a possibility that the child will be deformed or mentally deficient.

The widespread consensus has been expressed in specific recommendations of the American Law Institute in the United States and endorsed by the leading medical authorities. Furthermore, the American Civil Liberties Union is fighting for the abolition of all penalties connected with abortion. This influential organization claims that the present laws infringe on a woman's right to determine whether or when her body is to be used for procreation. The Civil Liberties Union, evidently, considers abortion a civil right of women.

As a result of all this, it is necessary for the Christian community to develop or review its own position concerning this subject and firm up its reaction. Wherever possible, Christian individuals must fearlessly and publicly express the witness of the Word of God concerning this vital matter. Christian young people and husbands and wives must formulate clear-cut attitudes that can guide them in connection with this vexing moral problem. Surely, people of Christian conscience must steadfastly oppose all laws that tend to downgrade the dignity of human life in whatever form that life appears. But even when liberal abortion laws exist, they may not be the final determination whether abortion is right or wrong for Christians. As a matter of fact, abortion for a wide variety of reasons is already legal in many places. But the question still remains whether or not those who know God's Word and understand it may ever consider abortion a real choice for them.

There are several factors that suggest that abortion is an abomination in the eyes of God. This of course would not hold true when it is necessary to save the life of the mother, but any abortion performed because of convenience to the individuals involved, for one reason or another, is the taking of a human life, an act that is condemned by the Bible.

The Bible indicates that all human life, even that which exists before birth, is of great dignity and supremely important in the eyes of God. Psalm 139 expresses the classic Biblical approach to the mystery of prenatal life when the writer says: "For thou didst form my inward parts, thou didst knit me together in my mother's womb. I praise thee, for thou art fearful and wonderful. Wonderful are thy works! Thou knowest me right well; my frame was not hidden from thee, when I was being made in secret, intricately wrought in the depths of the earth."

At this point, the Bible obviously indicates that the unborn enjoy the protection and loving direction of Almighty God. And this is so true, that later on, when full consciousness develops and an individual reflects on his origin, he may legitimately praise God because God has been with him, not only from birth, but also in that mysterious state before birth occurs. Even then all the potential for human individuality exists.

The question concerning precisely when a person becomes a person in the fullest sense of the term is hard to answer. But the psalmist does not assert that he was a fully formed person before his birth. He only indicates that already in the prenatal state, which may well be a prepersonal state, God was with him and caring for him. It is quite problematic to determine precisely when a person becomes a person, but there should be no argument that the prebirth forms of human life are at least human life, and indeed human life that is destined for full personhood if nothing intervenes.

Once it is clear that from the very earliest stages of prenatal life, we are dealing with human life that possesses all the potential for development into a fully formed human individual, the answers to the questions concerning abortion become quite clear in the light of the Bible. Often the question of abortion has been decided in terms of certain states of prenatal development, with abortion considered an option in the earliest months. Old English law tended to look on the unborn child differently before and after the so-called quickening. But gradually both law and medicine have begun to recognize that even quickening does not provide us with a proper standard of judgment that can determine when we are dealing with the dignity of human life. From the very earliest stages we are dealing with a unique form of human tissue that is destined, if unhindered, to become a real person, and this fact must condition our dealings with the unborn from the time of conception onward.

In an interesting article dealing with the legal rights of the unborn, Mr. Thomas F. Lambert, Jr., Editor in Chief of the American Trial Lawyers Association, has stated that "The . . . child in the womb should be treated as a person *for the purposes of tort law* whenever that is necessary to prevent injustice." He goes on to explain that, "In appropriate cases, the criminal law protects the unborn child and regards it as a separate entity." He also reports that "The laws of wills and property . . . considers the [unborn child] in being for purposes which are for its benefit and where justice so requires." Mr. Lamberts also rejects any arbitrary approach that suggests that an unborn child can expect the protection of the law after a certain stage of development and not before. He says, "It is emphasized that *for purposes of tort law,* protection of the child *in utero* may well commence from the moment of conception. . . ."

While Mr. Lamberts, in these statements, is speaking in the context of prenatal injury, this point of view is directly applicable to the moral problem confronting us in abortion as well. For abortion, obviously, is simply an especially severe form of prenatal injury, actually very malicious so far as the unborn is concerned. And it is interesting that this legal point of view concerning the rights of the unborn is substantiated by medical testimony which indicates that from the very beginning of existence in the mother, the unborn child is a separate individual entity that in no way can be considered a mere extension of the mother's life.

Once it is clear that unborn children are separate individual forms of human life, it is also clear that it is a serious crime to destroy these children, even at the earliest stage of their development. If it is necessary to use medical intervention to prevent eventual birth, the very use of these procedures is an admission that the unborn would have become a human being in the long run. This is as much a fact in the first trimester of development as in the last. Whatever we wish to say about personhood and the relation of the soul to the unborn, it is clear that, if the abortive medical procedures had not been employed, the being in question would have become a human personality in the fullest sense, who would have to be considered an image bearer of God.

This, after all, is the great teaching of the Bible concerning man. He is an image bearer of the living God, and the unborn child at the very least, must be

79

considered a potential image bearer of God. Once a person has been born, he has the right to live in God's world, to receive His benefits, and to respond to the saving grace of God revealed in Jesus Christ. And the unborn too must be viewed as someone who has these same rights potentially.

It becomes extremely dangerous for men, once conception has occurred, to begin to make decisions that lead to the destruction of the new life. Admittedly, often pregnancies are unwanted for one reason or another and many have occurred through the most unhappy of circumstances. But there are many people living useful lives today, whose origins were something less than ideal. That a child might possibly bring shame or inconvenience to its parents cannot be the principle used in determining whether the child shall be allowed birth or not. And even the case of deformity does not provide us with the right to take the extreme step of abortion. For who is to say that deformed people do not have the right to life? If this is true relative to those who are not yet born, what of those who are deformed and who consequently are the wards of the state in one way or another? Must they be killed, too?

And using abortion as it is frequently used — as a very efficient form of birth limitation — cannot be sanctioned by the slightest stretch of imagination. Those who call out the loudest for the repeal of all laws surrounding abortion often do so in the name of justice to the poor who have so many children. Without question, the problems in this connection are very grave, but the killing of unborn children is not the answer. The answer lies on a far deeper level, where the problem of poverty is faced squarely by a society and the proper changes and sacrifices are made to eradicate it. Once the beginning of a new life exists, it becomes sacred, and it is entitled to the protection society can give it.

Abortion — ten years ago this word could not have been used on television or the radio. But today it is becoming an issue and a possibility for many thousands of people. The best of families are finding themselves thinking about this new possibility. And that is why it is necessary for the full resources of the Word of God to be focused on this problem. Only then will we be able to see clearly through all the emotion that is being generated by those who suggest that abortion must not be considered a crime and must be made available to all who feel that it is necessary in their lives for one reason or another. We are told that change in abortion law will diminish the deaths now caused by criminal abortions and it will bestow upon women a new dignity, for it is essentially their right to choose whether their children will be allowed to be born or not.

But this is not a question of public health or of women's civil rights. It is a question of how a society looks upon human life in whatever form that life appears. Once conception has occurred, there exists an entity over which the mother and father and doctor no longer have the right of control. A new potential individual image bearer of the living God exists and now all of us must respond to that. What a pity it would be if there would be Christian people who would surrender to the emotionalism that often clouds this central issue and support public demands for the so-called reform of present abortion laws, or even worse, become involved in an abortion themselves because of their own selfish reasons.

We are apt to think that just because worldwide public opinion is swinging behind the so-called liberalization of abortion laws, therefore we should all consider this a real possibility. But no. Of course, there is a worldwide support of the new interest in killing unborn children. This is because there is a worldwide dehumanization of mankind that is the natural result of a total rejection of the Bible's declaration that man has been created in the image of God and is responsible to His creator. Man today thinks that he is merely an extension of the animal world, and this is why he can be so unmoved when he talks about the disposition of the unborn.

The great drive for changed attitudes toward abortion is being carried on in terms of humanitarian interests. There is something terrifying about this. Humanitarian interests? But which humans are consulted? Who represents the unborn who are destroyed in the process of saving humanity? Humanitarian interests indeed! Men turn to abortion when they discover that a new life stands in the way of their own selfish ambitions and desires, and complicates their world for one reason or another.

Without question, we have terrible problems today, but abortion is not the solution. People talk about rape, incest, poverty, deformity caused by drugs and the like in connection with the necessity for killing the unborn. Let's talk about all of these problems, seriously, hard-headedly and courageously and face them squarely. This is what our society needs desperately. It needs to review its miserable state in the light of God's Word and must find solutions that are compatible with the Bible's high view of humanity. But let's not talk about killing human life as the solution to everything.

I don't want to call abortion murder. Certainly it is

not murder in the first or second degree, for the human life killed is not a human person in the fullest sense of the term. But abortion is a serious crime unless it is done to save a mother's life. While it is not murder, it is the expression of the deepest perversity of human nature which always tries to eliminate everything that gets in its way. Men are willing to kill if they can't get what they want. And abortion is an expression of this perverse willingness.

A society that refuses to insist that abortion is a crime against humanity aborts its own future. And those who choose the way of abortion as the solution to their personal problems sin against the Almighty Creator who gave all of us our mysterious beginning.

10

The Family Altar

The altar has been a focal point of religious experience since time began. In Old Testament times the Israelites met God at the altar. When the altar lay in ruin, Israel's spiritual life was at low ebb.

Family worship is often referred to as the family altar. Regular and vital family worship is often a sign of a spiritually healthy family.

However, not every one is certain that family worship is important. Some think that it is too time-consuming for a family to read the Bible together and pray. Some do not have family worship because they honestly don't want to prejudice their children in favor of the Christian faith. They say, "When Johnny grows up, he must decide for himself what he believes." But of course, most people don't have it because they do not have any faith in the Bible and they don't know how to pray. One thing is certain: if parents are not absolutely sure that family worship is good and necessary, they are not going to bother with it.

Why are there still families who have family worship in their homes? Because there are still families who believe the Word of God which tells them that family worship is very important indeed. The Bible announces over and over again that parents are responsible for telling their children about God and about His great works. For example, look at Psalm 78.

This Psalm is full of the saving acts of God as He cared for His people Israel. All these facts are given with the instructions that parents are required to tell their children about them so that they will serve the Lord. This is what we read: "He [the Lord] established a testimony in Jacob, and appointed a law in Israel, which he commanded our fathers, that they should make them known to their children; that the next generation might know them, the children yet unborn, and arise and tell them to their children" (vv. 5, 6).

Obviously, in the Old Testament at least, God did not expect children to find out about Him when they became men, but He expected them to grow up with the knowledge of God which they had received from their fathers. The New Testament is no different. The promises of salvation were frequently directed to parents and their children. This was not because the children of believing parents were saved automatically because of some condition within their blood or in their genes. But the promises came to parents and their children because the whole Bible presupposes that Christian parents will be busy showing their children the wonderful works of God.

That is the reason we need family worship so badly. Parents will then have the opportunity to tell their children about God's saving love revealed in Jesus Christ. If you really believe on the Lord Jesus Christ, how can you fail to make opportunities within your family to tell your children about Him? Do you want them to learn about Jesus from somebody else? If you do, then most likely you haven't been very much impressed with Jesus yourself. Family worship is a must so that children can learn about God's salvation from their parents.

That's the "why" of family worship; one must also consider the "when." When should you have your family worship? It seems most natural to incorporate family worship into mealtimes. There are many practical reasons for this. First of all, that is the time when your family is together — at least they should be if your home is reasonably well run. In the second place, there is something very appropriate about worshiping God in connection with your mealtime. Many people feel instinctively that they should thank God for their food and ask His blessing on it. After all, we are not dogs who attack their food when it is set before them, but we are persons and we receive our food from a Person, God. We should acknowledge that. First Timothy 4:4, 5 says, "For everything created by God is good, and nothing is to be rejected if it is received with thanksgiving; for then it is consecrated by the word of God and prayer." Jesus gave thanks before He ate His food, and we should follow His example.

Eating a meal is not just an accidental event in life, it is related to the very essence of life itself. It is not a coincidence that one of the sacraments of the Christian church is a holy meal. God sanctifies all our meals when we thank Him for His food. And when the meal is over, there is an opportunity to think about the Giver of every good and perfect gift. You might like to have family worship at another time, but I think that in the long run you will find mealtime the most convenient and also, in certain ways, the most appropriate time for family worship.

Now comes the important question: How do you go about it? This question is not really more important than the others, but there are many, many people who would like to have family worship, but they don't have it because they don't know how to go about it. Perhaps a suggestion for a possible liturgy for family worship will help you in your home.

The first element of family worship is the prayer of thanksgiving before the meal. This can be a very simple prayer that recognizes God's care in our lives and asks Him to bless the food He has provided.

The second element of family worship is the reading of the Bible. After the meal is over, the father, who should be the leader in family worship, should read from the Bible something that is useful for his family. Some families begin at the beginning of the Bible and work through it systematically. This is a good idea so long as one is careful not to read those parts of the Bible that are not really meant for family worship. For example, the tedious family trees you find in the Bible, certain chapters that deal with especially gruesome sins, and the rather detailed prophecies you find sometimes, are not particularly useful when read in family worship. It is the father's responsibility, or the mother's in the father's absence, to see to it that the portions read are meaningful. This will mean that sometimes it will be necessary to make a short explanation of the passage read.

To make these Bible readings as meaningful as possible, sometimes the father may ask one of the children to read or he may ask his wife. But whoever reads must understand that the material must be read reverently and intelligently. There is no magic in the *words* of the Bible. Families are not sanctified by a few holy words read at the end of the meal. Nor is it always necessary to read the Bible exclusively. Sometimes it's good to use a Bible story book for the children's sakes. Many variations are possible, but all of them should be related to the Bible itself and should contribute to your understanding of this book and to your children's appreciation of it.

The final element of the liturgy of family worship is the closing prayer. Sometimes families eliminate this because they think that one prayer at mealtimes is enough. Perhaps it is, but the closing prayer is quite different from the first one. The first is simply a prayer of thanksgiving. The second is the prayer that concludes family worship and it may well be more general. The second prayer provides the family with an opportunity to remember their own needs more specifically. Perhaps the children can be asked if they have something special they would like their father or mother to pray for. Perhaps every member of the family will want to participate in this closing time of prayer. It's a good time to remember the sick friend down the street. It's a good time to remember the needs of the church. It's a good time to pray for religious radio broadcasts. In any case, it is this closing prayer that provides the opportunity for the family to bring its needs before Christ and it teaches every member to be prayerfully interested in the needs of others.

It is very simple, really. There are all kinds of variations you can make on this liturgy of family worship. Some families customarily learn the hymns of the church and the stately psalms together as part of their worship. There are many things you can do to make family worship significant and interesting. There is no reason why you cannot have this kind of worship each time the family is met together. It will not become boring, so long as the parents are true believers who are wise in dealing with their children and sincere when they speak about spiritual things. Of course, this kind of worship should never be very long, and it shouldn't be very formal. But this is the main thing: It should not be missing from your family.

So then, that is the "why," the "when," and the "how" of the family worship you should have in your home. Some may say, "Why, we can't begin to have that kind of family worship in our home. We would have to change so many things. The way it is now, Johnny has to go here and Jane has to go there, and sometimes Dad is gone a couple of nights in a row, and even Mother is busy with all kinds of things that often make mealtimes pretty haphazard. It is quite an accomplishment to get some food in front of everybody, but to think that a mother has time to sit down in the middle of the day with her children and pray and read the Bible with them, and to think that the family can sit calmly together long enough to have family prayers in the evening is pretty ridiculous. Oh, of course, sometimes we have friends in, and then we sit a long time at our meal. But to have family worship at mealtime is just a little bit impossible."

That is exactly the way it is. For many families some changes are going to have to be made if they are going to have family worship. But these changes would be the best thing in all the world for those families. We can become quite indignant sometimes about the juvenile delinquency we hear about, and we can be upset because of rising divorce rates, but if we are not willing to make our homes truly Christian homes, we might as well hold our tongues and save our breath. Do you really think that a husband and wife can seriously consider divorce when they have been engaged in family worship together along with their children? Do you think that marriages like that can break up at the slightest provocation? Of course not. The reason so many marriages are so brittle is because the association between the husband and wife and their children has no *spiritual* dimension.

And why do you think it is that so many young people today seem to be rebelling against minimum Christian principles? They don't know Christ, and the reason they don't is because they never met Him in their homes. Oh, their family is a Christian family all right — they are members of some church in the community. Every Christmas and every Easter and occasionally throughout the rest of the year they all dress up and march into church and sit there looking attentive. They sing lustily and after the service they all shake the minister's hand, and he is so glad to see them. But they have never learned to bring their common needs to Jesus' feet in prayer. Most of our young people are not rebelling against *Christianity* at all. They have just never been introduced to it by their fathers and their mothers.

If you don't have family worship in your home, won't you think about this matter very seriously? You owe it to yourself and to your children. In fact, you owe it to your *nation* to think about this matter, because a nation is only as strong as its homes, and its homes are only as strong as the family worship found within them.

Jesus Christ is the Savior of all those who repent of their sins and confess that He is their Redeemer and Lord. When He saves them He gives them wonderful blessings. One of the greatest blessings of all is this: He takes their homes and makes them holy.

11
Children Are People Too

Many parents would agree that some knowledge of the Bible is beneficial for their children. The Bible has some very pointed things to say to children. For example, one of the Ten Commandments says, "Honor your father and your mother. . . ." Another good verse for children to learn early is this one, found in Ephesians 6: "Children, obey your parents in the Lord, for this is right." No doubt one of the reasons Sunday schools often flourish even though adults may not be too interested in church attendance is that most people feel that the sooner children learn texts like this, the better for everyone.

But it is very sad that many parents who depend upon the Bible to set their children straight are not willing to listen to it themselves. Many parents who get all upset when Bible reading is removed from public schools and the like, seldom pay any attention to the Bible. The Bible has some very pointed things to say to them too. Our society will not be strong until both children and their parents are living their lives in the light of God's revelation, until both children and their parents live in obedience to God's Word.

If parents don't take the Bible seriously, it doesn't take long before their children begin to see through their conduct. If you say to your child when he's young, "Now, Johnny, you must be a good boy because

God wants you to be," while you keep showing Johnny that you personally don't care about what God's Word is saying, your son, if he's of average intelligence, is going to stop listening to God quite soon. He is going to follow your example, and you really cannot blame him for that. God has a message that is not only designed for children in Sunday school, but also for their parents. It is very important that parents start listening to what God is saying to them along with their children. That is the only way our homes can be strong, and that is the only way our nation can be strong as well.

The Bible can help parents in many ways, but one of the most important is this: It helps parents think about their children properly. Actually the Bible's message concerning children is a very simple one, but it is extremely profound. The Bible tells us that *children are people too*. We often forget this. We tend to think of children as junior members of the human race. We have all kinds of categories that we put them into. We talk about the terrible two-year-olds and the fearsome four-year-olds. When they go to school we talk about them in terms of their being second graders or fifth graders, and finally we lump them all together and call them teen-agers. Adults frequently feel they know how children in all of these categories are supposed to act. In any case, we often forget that they are people, that they are just as important as adults. We must take them seriously as individuals, because God takes them seriously. The Bible knows nothing about these pigeon-holes into which we place our children. It describes them as full-fledged, important people who must be treated with consideration and respect.

This is nowhere more clear than in the sixth chapter of Ephesians where the Bible tells children to obey their parents. Immediately following this command to children, the Bible says, "Fathers, do not provoke your children to anger, but bring them up in the discipline and instruction of the Lord" (v. 4). The Bible takes the anger of children seriously, much more seriously than we might be inclined to do. If our children are aggravated or edgy, if they cry a great deal, we are not very ready to agree that it is our fault. It's theirs. They are cutting teeth, or they didn't get enough sleep. As they grow older, we explain their surliness by remembering that, after all, they are teen-agers now. Of course, each one of these explanations is useful so far as it goes, but the Bible reminds us that parents themselves can often be the cause of their children's problems.

When adults have toothaches or headaches, they expect to be treated with consideration. Don't you think that when the Bible tells us that we may not provoke children to anger, it means, at the very least, that we must treat them with respect and consideration? This does not mean, of course, that we must not be firm with them frequently and even punish them when necessary. The Bible makes very clear elsewhere that parents are responsible for correcting their children. But while the parent does all this, he must remember that his child is a person who must be treated with love and respect.

The Biblical approach to the training of children will not be achieved unless parents understand the Bible's total point of view with respect to the family and the significance of children. Today we consider good those things which provide individual adults with the greatest satisfaction and pleasure. Because of this, children are often considered a burden — they are little people who keep getting in their parents' way and generally they make life less than fun for others. The Bible has an entirely different point of view. It never views society as a collection of individual adults who must be made happy one way or another, but it views society as an organization that is made up of families. In the Bible, the welfare of the family is important, and the welfare of individuals is achieved in the degree that the families are healthy and happy.

Even God's great promises of salvation are not given to individuals as individuals, but to individuals as members of families. When God promised His salvation to Abraham in the Old Testament, His promise embraced Abraham's family and generations still to be born. This is what God said, "And I will establish my covenant between me and you and your descendants after you throughout their generations for an everlasting covenant, to be a God to you and to your descendants after you" (Genesis 17:7). In simple English, God said, "Abraham, I make an everlasting promise to you that I will be your God and the God of your children." And that is the reason why Abraham's children had to bear the mark of God's promise, the mark of circumcision, already when they were babies. God did not work with Abraham alone, but His promise of salvation embraced Abraham's children too.

It's amazing, but true: God still deals with believers *and their children* today. Now that Jesus Christ has come, has died, risen again, and now reigns in heaven, God still works the same way. We see that in the New Testament. Even in situations in which the promise of salvation was announced in a highly charged emotional context, the promise did not fail to include a reference to its significance for families. Take the case of the Philippian jailer, for example, as recorded in Acts 16. Paul and Silas were in prison. Suddenly

94

at night there was an earthquake, and the prison doors broke open. The jailer, thinking all had escaped, seized a sword to kill himself. The apostle Paul restrained him. The distraught jailer asked, 'Men, what must I do to be saved?" Paul and his companion answered, "Believe in the Lord Jesus Christ, and you will be saved, you and your house" (v. 31).

The Bible tells us that the jailer was baptized that very night — "with all his family" (v. 33). Baptism, in the New Testament, took the place of the sign of circumcision as the mark of God's promise. It is very important to remember that baptism was frequently administered to entire households. One writer declares, ". . . Baptism must have been very frequent in the days of the apostles. But only some twelve instances are actually recorded. . . . It is quite illuminating that at least three of these instances refer to household baptism. Every consideration would point to the conclusion that household baptism was a frequent occurrence in the practice of the church in the apostolic days."

If God's promises of grace included children in the Old Testament period and if His promises are no less generous today, then children become very important people — some of the most important people we will ever know. Once, during the course of His earthly ministry, Jesus made this perfectly clear. In Luke 18 we read this about Jesus: "Now they were bringing even infants to him that he might touch them; and when the disciples saw it, they rebuked them. But Jesus called them to him, saying, 'Let the children come to me, and do not hinder them; for to such belongs the kingdom of God. Truly, I say to you, whoever does not receive the kingdom of God like a child shall not enter it' " (vv. 15-17). In Matthew 18 we find a similar record of Jesus and the children. Here we read: 'Whoever receives one such child in my name receives me; but whoever causes one of these little ones who believe in me to sin, it would be better for him to have a great millstone fastened round his neck and to be drowned in the depth of the sea" (vv. 5, 6).

Obviously Jesus Christ wanted to demonstrate, so that there could be no question about it, that God is not impressed by the distinctions we make between adults and children. We tend to think that a person is not really important until he has grown up, has received his education, and has become financially independent. Before they settle down and become just like their parents, we tend to think of children as problems of one kind or another. Look at all the articles and books that are written about children and their problems. Much of it is necessary, but it is far out of proportion to the actual contribution to mankind's predicament children make. Surely, our children and our teen-agers and our young people have problems today, but ask any minister who is an honest pastor and he will tell you the parents have problems too, deep and soul-searing problems. Parents often want their children to learn how to pray, but how many of *them* pray? They want their children to know the Bible, but how many of *them* ever read it? They want their children to be pure and honest, but the *parents* are not always so pure themselves. They don't want their children to drink or smoke, but, of course, once you pass thirty — why, that's different.

In the sight of God, according to the Bible, children are full-fledged people and He wants their parents to remember that always. This means that if you have children, you must take them as seriously as you take your job and the people with whom you work. You must take your children as seriously as you take your golf or tennis or fishing. God presents you with your children and declares, "Never forget, these people are important to Me and they must be important to you. You may not make them angry. You may not make them secondary. You may not treat them with indifference any more than you may treat your wife, or your husband, or anyone else with indifference. You may not look upon them as a passing trial that fortunately someday will be lifted off your shoulders."

If anything in your life gets between you and your children, you must destroy it. You are responsible for your children's attitudes and if you fail your children, remember the words of Jesus: ". . . it were better for him that a millstone were hanged about his neck, and that he were drowned in the depth of the sea." God wants you to tell your children about the Lord Jesus Christ, and to bring them up in the nurture and admonition of the Lord.

This is why it is tragic that there are so many people today who want their children to receive religious training of one kind or another, but who are not willing to live in obedience to Jesus Christ themselves. When the Bible says, ". . . do not provoke your children to anger, but bring them up in the discipline and instruction of the Lord," it presupposes that the parents know the Lord Jesus Christ themselves. Ideally a husband and wife must both rejoice in their belief that Jesus Christ has died on Calvary's cross to take their sins away and they must both be dedicated to serving their Savior within their family. How can people possibly give their children the faith they need the most, if they don't have it themselves?

It takes more than the patience of Job and the wisdom of Solomon to raise your children properly today. It takes the grace of God to do it. Our children today are subjected to terrible pressures. The competition that exists today wears on them relentlessly. There are awesome forces that compel them to conform. Temptations to commit outright sin are everywhere. The parents must give them guidance. How can they really help them, if they do not point them to the Lord Jesus Christ? How can they help their children if they don't know how to pray for them? And how can they help their children if they do not know how to pray for themselves, if they are too proud to implore God to give them the wisdom necessary to be the kind of parents God wants them to be?

Children are real people and God is deeply concerned about them. That is what makes it so impressive when God gives children. Sometimes a young couple can be quite shaken when they discover that God is going to give them a child. They wonder what it is going to do to their finances and how it is going to change their lives. But really, finances and the busyness of a family — these are secondary matters. The really fearful thing about receiving children is this: God brings a new person into your life, a person, with all that that means. That person is going to be a part of your life every day from now on, until he begins his own family. That child will always be there, and you will be responsible to love him, and to guide him, always with respect for his personality. You will have to correct him and even punish him. But you may not provoke him to anger. And with all of this, God appoints you to be His prophet so that your children will learn the exciting story of salvation from your lips.

Who is sufficient for these things? No one, not even those who know the Lord and who confess that He is their Savior. Every parent, even the most pious and wise, must always feel remorse because he knows that he has failed his children, far too often. But the Christian parent can make a beginning and when he fails, he can go to God and ask God's forgiveness for Jesus' sake. But what is more, the Christian parent has this great advantage: God works in the hearts of children whose parents are Christians so that they understand their parents and their parents' failure. Finally the children and the parents stand together before the cross of Calvary and rejoice in the knowledge that Christ has covered all their sin through His precious blood.

The Christian faith is wonderful because it brings salvation to men, but it is even more wonderful because it brings salvation to *families*. This doesn't mean that every child of believing parents is saved automatically, but the Bible clearly states that God is pleased to reveal His glorious salvation to parents and their children. Because of this, the responsibility placed upon the parents is indescribably great. May God grant that we may return to the Lord so that our families may be Christian. Such families can make our country strong.

12

Heart Failure

Of all the plaintive wails hanging over our smog enshrouded cities, few are more touching than the dismayed cry, "What has happened to our young people?" Everybody — and I mean everybody who for one reason or another doesn't consider himself a member of the younger generation — everybody is shocked and horrified. The middle-aged generation is shocked by the excesses of the campus. But quite apart from excesses, the young in their ordinary, relatively wholesome behavior are swinging on a different wave length. Their form of dress, the music they like, and their easygoing attitudes towards sex cause their parents and their uncles and aunts no end of consternation.

Now, all the criticism of young people today is not justified. In some cases, the younger generation is doing remarkably well. One college administrator has said, "For all the criticism of this generation, I think the kids are more serious now than they have ever been." Such statements are no doubt true, but obviously something is dreadfully wrong when undisciplined, revolutionary youths turn the campuses of large universities into armed camps, when students demand the right to express themelves in obscenity and engage in licentious conduct without reprimand, and when seventh graders "trade barbiturates in home-rooms and smoke marijuana during lunch." Something has gone horribly wrong, too, when you discover that your child, a brand new teen-ager, can gaze unmoved on the most shocking violence, and smile wisely at lewdness and vulgarity.

Maybe the snowballing headlines that announce that we've got a full-blown crisis on our hands will make most of us a bit more willing to listen seriously to the answer to the question, "Why has this happened?" There is an answer. There is a reason for the big split between the generations. There is a reason why a multitude of parents are shocked and horrified by their children's behavior while the children are cynical and condescending when they deal with their parents. There is a reason for all of this, and maybe now we are ready to say, "Yes, I guess that's right. . . ."

Maybe we would even be willing to listen to the Bible's wisdom on this subject. We don't open the Bible often, but in times of emergency, people have been known to do so. Now that our society is in the grips of an emergency, it would be good to look at what the Bible says. And the Bible says something very pointed about the behavior of older children and adults. It says that the way people act when they grow up is determined by the way they were trained when they were young. Proverbs 22:6 says it very plainly: "Train up a child in the way he should go: and when he is old, he will not depart from it."

What the Bible is saying, simply and practically, is just this: the way children are trained in the home will determine how they think and act later. Child training determines adult behavior. Why are our children the way they are? Just look at the homes they came from, and you will know.

This is tremendously important. This rule from the Bible should not plunge us all into despair so that we all go around with guilty consciences, young people proclaiming how bad they are and their parents smiting their breasts because they have made them that way. This rule from the Bible, child training determines adult behavior, can rehabilitate our families and give direction to those of us who are just starting off. The young people should be especially encouraged, because if they follow the Bible's rule they will have a chance to do something fine and good for their children. Unless the home becomes a child training center again, designed to furnish the child with rich, wholesome experiences, we are in for mountains of trouble in the years ahead. On the other hand, those who listen carefully to the Bible's advice will contribute to the healing of some of the ugly wounds that fester within our society.

There is not going to be any significant improvement in the quality of social life until parents face up to their own responsibilities for forming their children in the early years within the home. When we survey the shambles of our times, we frequently criticize the schools. But we must not forget that the home has far more potential for forming children than the schools have. We must remember that one of the reasons the schools are so exceptionally effective in forming children today is that they fill the vacuum left when the parents shirk their own responsibilities for their children.

Recently it has been documented that intelligence is very dependent upon the environment in the home. We are told that one-half of all growth in human intelligence takes place between the ages of one and four. These are ages when a child is formed almost exclusively by the conditions that prevail within his home. Another 30 percent of intelligence develops between the fourth and eighth years. These are also years when a child is still under the control of the home. In an article, "Kindergarten is Too Late," Esther P. Edwards has stressed that early social and family circumstances provide the child's most basic storehouse of learning experience.

If you have growing children in your home, or if you have just welcomed a baby into your family, this information is frightening. Don't think that you've got a couple of decades to influence your children one way or another. You have just a few years — 80 percent of their intelligence will be formed by the time they are eight years old! And by the time your children go to kindergarten, much of their future development has already been programed by what you have said and done and by how you have reacted to their needs. The Bible has emphasized this all along. The Bible has always declared that the home is the place where people are formed. If we do not get busy and do the job from the very beginning, our children will be in trouble. And when a whole nation of parents refuses to face up to their parental responsibilities, the whole nation will become sick and will get sicker with every new year.

"Train up a child in the way he should go: and when he is old, he will not depart from it." This fundamental rule laid down by the Bible, and confirmed by what we know today, helps us understand why things don't seem to be working out for us anymore so far as training our children is concerned. The fact is that parents are just *not* training their children anymore. They are not doing the job. Professor Urie Bronfenbrenner, professor of child development and family relationships at Cornell University, has said, "Children used to be brought up by their parents. It

103

may seem presumptuous to put that statement in the past tense. Yet it belongs to the past." In his article, "The Split Level American Family," he indicates how children today are generally influenced mainly by their peers and television. So far as the home is concerned, he points out that children are seldom there.

Now, this professor is telling us what most of us already know from everyday experience. Parents are turning their backs on their children. They bring them into the world and then seem willing to palm them off on anyone who will take care of them. Fathers are so intensely occupied with their work and their play they really never get to know their children. And mothers resent their obligations and flee the home as soon as possible.

This is disastrous. If a child cannot experience close association with his parents during his most formative years, he is deprived of a priceless necessity. What a responsibility a mother has! Reading to the children, playing with them, loving them, reprimanding them, teaching them to pray — all this is her high privilege and sometimes exasperating duty. It takes emotional and spiritual energy and a high level of mental and physical health to do the job. But it's worth the effort, no matter how dreary it sometimes becomes.

Fathers, too, have a far greater responsibility for the rearing of their children than they often realize. Of necessity they must be away often throughout the day. But any father who does not make sure that he is around his home on Sundays, giving his children the spiritual direction they need, is making a colossal mistake. Fathers must find ways to live as closely to their developing children as possible. Both the father and the mother must cooperate in providing their children with a home in which a treasury of rich, wholesome experiences grows, and the children receive useful equipment with which to face the world.

Specifically, both father and mother must cooperate in enforcing rules that will eliminate from the home those influences that can corrupt developing children. This means, at the very minimum, that television viewing must be controlled by the parents. The home in which the television screen is on most of the time, and children and parents watch one program after the other with little or no discrimination, is in serious trouble. Many homes are finding it increasingly necessary to demand that the television sets be off unless there is something *good for children*. And the *good for children* rating cannot be applied to the variety shows that mock holy things, and that present an unreal, amoral, violent view of life. It cannot be applied to all of the situation comedies either. And don't forget that the daytime soap operas can damage children just as much as mothers.

But this kind of direction and expression of parental responsibility is disappearing today. Our nation is experiencing family failure. And that is like heart failure. When the family fails, a nation's heart fails. Why is it? We all know that the Bible is right when it says that the key to the future lies in the way we deal with our children now. But why don't people pitch in and take hold and do the job that needs to be done in training their children?

If you read the whole Bible, you begin to see why the family is failing today. The Bible always portrays us in a relationship to God. This training of children is not a simple thing whereby you teach them to do this and you teach them not to do that. We referred to intelligence a little earlier in this chapter, but the training of a child involves more than his intelligence.

Look at your little two-year-old and four-year-old if you have one. Training that child involves molding every part of that little guy or that little gal. Emotions come into the picture. Love must accompany everything you do. And the spiritual life of the child is also involved. And your spiritual life is, too.

When the Bible says, "Train up a child in the way he should go . . ." it is talking first of all about spiritual things. From the very beginning your child must see that you know God through Jesus Christ and are trying to serve Jesus with your life. When you teach your child from that point of view, he learns how to pray, and he learns early that he is living in the sight of God.

I firmly believe that one of the main reasons parents have given up on the training of their children is that they aren't sure of themselves anymore. They don't know God, and they don't know Jesus Christ, and they do not have the Holy Spirit in their hearts. They do not have any real convictions about what life is all about. They themselves have never come to grips with the biggest issues of life. They don't know what they are and they don't know who God is. They never go to church, they never read the Bible, and they never pray. They don't have anything to give their children and they know it. Why not let the television set bring them up, or why not let the schools try to do the job in their way, or why not let your children's friends become the greatest influence in their lives? Why not? The parents have nothing to give.

According to the Bible, the only parents who will be able to train their children properly are those who have settled their own spiritual problems and have responded in faith to the Bible's message. Obviously, parents who have succumbed to the prevailing ideas that suggest that there is no God and man is part of nature, have no balance in their own lives. They cannot be expected to give their children proper direction. With their naturalistic view of this world and of themselves, their own performance will most likely be disappointing, and they will not be able to serve as useful examples to their children.

But those who know that the God of the Bible lives and that He has been revealed perfectly in Jesus Christ, live in a world that is solid and secure. Their own lives are built on the firm foundation faith in Jesus can give. They receive their children as gifts from God, and they know that the greatest task they have in all the world is to be good parents to those children. Because they are sure of themselves, and know the kind of conduct God expects of them, they are able to help their children find their way through the maze of contradictory elements in our modern world.

Such parents are also continually fortified by the great promises God has given to believers and their children. It is so striking that the Bible persistently assures those who believe, that their children shall benefit richly from the faith of the parents.

Those who believe in Jesus are saved, and their sons and daughters, too. This does not mean that the children must not themselves come to the point of personal faith in Jesus, but it does mean that the parents have the spiritual power to set their children on the way to a useful, meaningful life. They can train them in many things because they are not afraid to train them in the things of God.

There is only one medicine that can possibly help in connection with the great social crisis that grips our world right now. It is the medicine God furnishes in

His Word, the holy Bible. Here we meet Jesus, and here we have the opportunity to bow in faith before Him. Men and women who acknowledge that this Jesus is their Savior and their Lord are able to contribute something to the solution of the ugly problems that now drive us to distraction. They can have families in which children experience the security that deep and abiding love can bring. They can have families in which the children learn that Jesus is their Redeemer and they must serve Him constantly.

Family failure is the failure of a nation's heart. Who can deny that our nation is now gasping for breath as it tries to shake off the agony caused by this awesome sickness? And where do you and your children fit into all of this? Are you a part of the problem, or will you, through God's great grace, help mend the torn fabric of these times?

Believe on the Lord Jesus Christ and you will be saved, and your house. Then you will be able to train your children in the way they should go, and when they grow up they will not disappoint you.

13

What the World Needs Now Is Authority

If you want to get a rise out of people nowadays just bring up the subject of law and order. Everyone has their strong opinion about how they would deal with lawless people. Sometimes public speakers seem to be competing with each other to see who can talk the toughest. And, occasionally, really brutal remarks break into print. For example, an article on the American middle class recently reported that at least one veteran of one of America's wars said that if he would be allowed to use his old M-1 rifle he could take care of the rioters on the streets pretty quickly.

Now, when there is such a consistently violent reaction to this subject, we should be a little suspicious. Why are these people so uptight about crime in the streets and the general lawlessness in the land? There is no doubt that most of the major cities in the world are facing a problem (with the exception of those where the poor are just too starved to cause anyone any trouble). But the seriousness of the problem does not explain the extremely energetic and often hysterical way people talk about law and order.

Whenever people get this excited about problems in society it is most likely because the roots of the problems lie rather close to their own lives and they suspect that this is so. For example, some of the people who are so utterly indignant about pornography are people who feel especially threatened by pornography because of their own perverse interest in it. And so, too, there is good reason to believe that one of the reasons people are so excited about the fact that there is so much lawlessness and so little order today is that they know that the origins of the problem lie very close to home. The very people who cannot understand how rioters can burn down a city, sometimes know within their hearts that in their own less obvious way they are destroying people's property, too. They break the law, too, though their lawlessness is more under cover and less noticeable.

The breakdown of law and the high incidence of disorder in our society is, obviously, related to the general lack of respect that prevails everywhere today. And much of the reason so many people are up in arms is that they feel a sense of guilt themselves because they know that they themselves are contributing to this lack of respect. Why do people hate police officers, why do students protest and riot, and why do antisocial crimes flourish? Certainly one of the main reasons is that so many people respect no one but themselves, and often they don't even do that. The cause of this widespread lack of respect is this: We are ignoring the Bible's description of the family. For according to the Bible, the family is the heart of all society and once respect disappears within it, men's respect for each other and for themselves will disappear everywhere. It is as simple as that. People are so exceptionally excited about the breakdown of society because they feel the ground breaking beneath their own feet. Our homes are sick. Lawlessness and disorder flow like burning lava from homes that have forgotten God and His Word.

There is a very interesting document in the Old

Testament called the Ten Commandments. These simple statements contain a description of the way God wants us to live. The first four of them deal with our relationship to God and tell us how we must worship Him, and the second group, consisting of the last six commandments, tell us how we must live with each other. They tell us how society must be governed and laid out. It is suicidal for a person to disregard the teaching of these commandments. It is also suicidal for a nation to disregard these teachings, for if it does, it will be overrun by great internal disorder. The first commandment in the second group talks about the home, which is the foundation of society.

Instead of wasting our breath telling others how we are going to shoot rioters, or how we are going to burn down the buildings of the landlords that oppress us, let us *listen* to the first of the commandments that should govern our social life: "Honor your father and your mother, as the Lord your God commanded you; that your days may be prolonged, and that it may go well with you, in the land which the Lord your God gives you" (Deuteronomy 5:16).

God here reveals that any description of society must begin with a discussion of the respect children must give their parents. The respect that is exercised within the family is not just something that makes the family a nicer place in which to live, but it is something that will make it possible for the whole nation to exist successfully. This is why the commandment to honor our parents contains a promise for prosperity within the nation, if it is obeyed. And notice carefully that God simply *commands* children to honor their parents. He does not discuss this and show them how it would be wise to honor their parents because the parents know more than the children, or

111

because they provide for the children. With this commandment, God simply *places* parents over their children. He *gives* them authority over their children. Authority — this is what we should do some thinking about. There is lack of respect in the land because few people recognize that there is such a thing as authority. Parents have authority because God has placed them over their children. And others have authority, too. If we could get this straight once again, there might be some hope for these wretched times.

The idea of authority is considered very, very square these days, especially when you relate the idea to a social institution as old-fashioned as the home. We still know what the word means in theory, at least, but we talk mostly about rights nowadays. Human rights *are* very important and we will never be through talking about them, but when they are discussed without reference to authority, anarchy results. We see that happening now. Exclusive emphasis on the rights of criminals with no corresponding emphasis on the authority of the state to enforce law is leading to an erosion of law enforcement. Emphasis on students' rights without corresponding emphasis upon the authority of an educational institution to determine what education must be is resulting in chaos on the educational scene. And an emphasis on the rights of children without a discussion of the authority of their parents is leading to a rapid breakdown of the home. It is right here, the loss of authority in the home, where all the other trouble starts. Once we stop talking about the authority parents have been given by God Himself, we lose its connection with other parts of our lives.

But haven't we come to the point where all of us are forced to consider that perhaps by eliminating God-given authority from our lives we have lost something essential? Isn't there now enough evidence to show us that unless we start talking about authority again, civilization could well be utterly destroyed? Of course, it is entirely possible that once the authority the Bible talks about is removed, totalitarian forms of authority will grow increasingly stronger. But totalitarianism is disastrous, too. The harsh, brutal statements politicians are making these days about the way they will handle the problem of law and order are frightening. Sometimes they border on the cute, but when they talk of meeting lawlessness with more lawlessness, the prospect they paint is utterly horrible. Only a recovery of the Bible's description of authority and of where it starts will help us now.

I guess we would all admit that we need help and something must be done to restore respect and change men so that they will not continue in their rebellious rejection of everything that is fine and good in our world. But do we really want to talk about authority? We have had our fill of authority, and freedom is so sweet we would rather experiment with it a few more years to see if some good could possibly come. The idea of authority is cold and forbidding.

It *is* cold and forbidding when you start talking about it from the top down, when you start talking about the authority government has and then work down from there. But the Bible doesn't start there. It starts with the family. And if we also start here and see what we can do about restoring authority to parents and respect for parents among children, we will find that we are talking about something that is very wholesome, warm, and good.

For, when the Bible places parents over their children and commands children to honor them, it does this for very practical reasons. God did not arrange society this way so that parents would have an exalted position over their children, and would always be assured that their children would serve them and look after them. The Ten Commandments are not just trying to insure that the establishment will be preserved. When God told the children to honor their parents, He used this arrangement in order to make certain that the children would have the fear of the Lord in their lives.

According to the Bible, parents are not just the biological origin of their children. They are charged with the responsibility of communicating the knowledge of God. They must help their children know and serve God.

In the sixth chapter of the Book of Deuteronomy, the fact that God wants parents to instruct their children in the fear of the Lord is brought out. This is what we read: "Hear, O Israel: The Lord our God is one Lord, and you shall love the Lord your God with all your heart, and with all your soul, and with all your might. And these words which I command you this day shall be upon your heart; and you shall teach them diligently to your children, and shall talk of them when you sit in your house, and when you walk by the way, and when you lie down, and when you rise" (vv. 4-7). These words come almost immediately after God's command that children honor their parents. They must, indeed — and their parents must honor God. Children are commanded to honor their parents, but the parents are commanded to keep God's commandments in their hearts and teach them to their children.

The authority arrangement which God laid down within the family is not just a convenience. It is also a teaching arrangement designed to insure that the knowledge of God will not disappear and parents and their children will continue to serve their God. And with this we see why this is so important to us today. Authority must be revitalized within the family once again, but it must be an authority that is nurtured and honored so that the children within the family will know who God is and how He must be served.

What this all comes down to is this: Before we become all excited about the breakdown of law and order in society in general, we had better take a long hard look at our own lives. What is happening in your home, and if you are young and plan to establish a home of your own some day, what kind of a home do you intend to set up? If your home or the home you intend to have some day is going to be a home where the name of God is never heard, except perhaps in profanity, where there is no interest whatever in knowing more about God and about His only begotten Son, the Lord Jesus Christ, then you might as well save your breath when it comes to your talk about lawlessness within the land.

If children never have the opportunity to learn about God and about His Son Jesus from their parents, what can you possibly expect from them when they get older? If they never learn that God is the Creator and that in Jesus Christ He can become the Lord of their lives, why should they ever be impressed with the authority of a school administrator or a police officer or a government official! If people never learn the fear of God, they will never properly respect the people who exercise authority in our world. Once a nation loses its grip on the knowledge of God, the doors are open for anything to happen.

When parents represent God and teach the knowledge of God to their children, the foundations of an orderly society are laid. Our children must understand that authority comes from God — that He gives it to parents first of all, and then to other agencies in society so that they can protect the home. Only when we understand that authority comes from God can we understand that it exists for our profit and well-being. The Bible reveals so clearly that the God who gives authority to parents is the God who saves men through His love. He is a loving God, and He has revealed His love in Jesus Christ who died on Calvary's cross so that all who believe in Him would not perish but have everlasting life.

If young people grow up resenting authority and thinking that authority is just a harsh expression of the selfishness of the middle class or of the establishment, then they will certainly become rebels. But when they respect their parents for the authority God has given them, they will know that on the long term the exercise of authority will be for their eventual good.

We are in desperate trouble today. The conditions in our world are nearly intolerable. Fear grips people everywhere and we are reaping the fruits of our rebellion. The rebellion of the present moment begins in our homes where parents refuse to listen to the message of the Word of God and humble themselves before God's authority. Parents have turned their back on God in so many instances, and when it comes to their children's religious position, they say, "Oh, we wouldn't want to influence Johnny. When he is old enough he will just have to decide for himself what he will believe." What they fail to see is that, with their skepticism and flagrant violation of God's law, they are influencing Johnny every day, whether they want to or not, and the possibility of his ever fearing

116

God is very slim. Then they wonder why their son finally becomes one of the many rebels who want to see the world turned upside down, even if they don't have anything to put in its place.

All the boisterous, inhumane talk that explodes whenever the subject of law and order comes up is often an evasion of the great issue behind it all. Those who cringe in horror when they see crime erupting, must examine their own lives and their homes and ask what they are doing to show others that God rules and He must be obeyed. We should stop shouting and becoming angry. We should just repent and acknowledge that we have all strayed far from the Word of God and from the fear of God.

Law and order rests on a sure foundation only where men believe in the Lord Jesus Christ and teach their children to fear the Lord. God-fearing people with God-fearing children are the key to peace in our day. Repent and believe the Gospel.

14

The Child Stealers

Crimes committed against children are the most vicious, and the punishments prescribed for them are the most severe. Society shows little mercy when it apprehends a kidnaper. Stealing children is one of the most reprehensible violations of human life and society.

But child stealing is going on all the time. Everyone who is interested in children and everyone who is interested in the future of his country should be well aware of the child stealing that has become so common, we are not shocked by what is happening.

Before one can discuss child stealing, it is necessary to determine to whom children belong.

There are essentially two possible answers to this intriguing question. The first answer is the most obvious one: Children belong to their parents. If you have children, you probably thought that everyone assumes that your children belong to you. But there is another answer to the question, to whom do children belong? This answer has achieved widespread acceptance. It is this: Children belong to the community. To put it just a little differently: children belong to the state.

If we look at modern life closely, we discover that men seem to be assuming more and more that children are actually the property of the state. The state

118

claims the right to determine the goals of children's lives and trains them to achieve these goals. The state expresses its ownership of children through state control of education. The schools of the nation need not necessarily reflect the points of view of the parents, but they should reflect the broad points of view which all citizens are supposed to share in common. As a matter of fact, whenever parents assert their right to determine the quality and nature of their children's education in a way that contradicts the state's ideas, the parents rather quickly experience coercion through state power.

Many of us know how efficiently the state exercises control of children in a totalitarian society. Nazi Germany was skilled at turning very young children against their parents by means of youth organizations and sinister employment of the educational system.

But even within the free nations today, there are policies in effect that tend in the direction of that taken by totalitarian regimes. In the United States, the educational establishment is becoming an increasingly dominant force in society. A psychiatrist who recently spent a week in meetings with the National Educational Association reports that top educational strategists are beginning to think of educational institutions as large warehouses in which students are stored from four and five years of age until they can be turned loose in the adult world. And the educators, usually supported by the impressive power of the state, feel responsible to work with the child during that period of time so that the "proper" finished product is produced.

The increasing emphasis upon preschool training is also part of the trend to get children away from the parents and into an environment which will insure that they will turn out to be the kind of people the nation, not the parents particularly, but the kind of people the *nation* wants them to be.

Now if children do belong to the community as a whole — that is, to the state — the gradual increase of state control over child development is good and proper. But if children do not belong to the state, this rapidly accelerating process amounts to child stealing. The fact that the process is so vast and pervasive should not blind us to what is happening. When children are removed from those who properly have the responsibility for their development, the long term results will be disastrous for the children, and consequently, for the entire country.

There can be no question about the Bible's judgment regarding the present state of affairs. So far as the Bible is concerned, children belong to the parents. The parent/child relationship is sacred and is most vital to the health of the total society. Everything within our world must serve this relationship. The family, the home, is absolutely important. Therefore, children are told to look to their parents for direction. Every other instrument used for their further development must be in line with the basic concerns, convictions, and ideals of the home.

In Ephesians 6, there are specific statements directed to children which highlight the parent/child relationship. "Children, obey your parents in the Lord, for this is right. 'Honor your father and mother' (this is the first commandment with a promise), 'that it may be well with you and that you may live long on the earth.' Fathers, do not provoke your children to anger, but bring them up in the discipline and instruction of the Lord."

These words from the New Testament are an extension of the commandments directed toward the family in the Old Testament. The Ten Commandments are very concerned to guard the sanctity of the family. They guard marriage itself by prohibiting adultery. One of the commandments tells children they are to honor their father and mother. Psalm 78, in the Old Testament, is a lengthy description of what the parents should tell their children about God and about His way with His people. The writer of the Psalm says "[God] established a testimony in Jacob, and appointed a law in Israel, which he commanded our fathers to teach to their children; that the next generation might know them, the children yet unborn, and arise and tell them to their children, so that they should set their hope in God, and not forget the works of God, but keep his commandments" (vv. 5-7).

Remember, the Bible declares that the children belong to the parents who, in turn, receive their directives from God. The home is to be a dynamic center for child development where children learn about the basic issues of life and about God and His way with this world. The parents' responsibilities in child training are awesome and grave. Nevertheless these responsibilities are inescapable and they may not be passed on or surrendered to any general community agency that offers to do the job on behalf of the parents.

But in spite of the Bible's clear declaration that the children belong to the parents, the great process of child stealing continues with no relief in sight. How can this be? It occurs because there is a conspiracy whereby the parents actually cooperate in the process and gradually surrender the children to the community as a whole. The fact is, the very quality of parenthood is deteriorating rapidly. Parents are afraid of their children. They are frustrated by the boogieman of the generation gap. What is worse, they are un-

121

willing to give their children useful counsel about things that really matter. Once they have brought their children into the world, they feel helpless and there is an unconscious relief when a large public agency volunteers to take over the training of their children.

The sad truth is that parents are not willing to fight to retain possession of their children. Oh, they want custody of their children, indeed. They want them around the house for a few years so long as they are reasonably well behaved, but they are not jealously concerned to retain their parental right to influence their children at the deepest level of their lives. They half believe, possibly they believe entirely, that the state, expressed in some of the large institutions within our society, the public school for instance, is capable of determining what is best for their children better than they are. Because parents are unsure of themselves and morally bankrupt in many instances, they are afraid to get on with the big job of being parents. So the state takes the children, and the parents give them up without a struggle.

How is this trend of stealing children to be reversed? I don't think it can be. But it is possible, here and there, in this family and in that family, and in certain communities, to retain possession of the children and create pockets of resistance. This must be done, not just to fight the evil tendency to turn over child training to the state, but in order to provide our total society with groups of people who are able to make a useful contribution to our common life in terms of the idealism and the faith that is a part of the glorious heritage of Christianity. You see, ultimately, the children who are turned over to the state for education and training end up being deprived children.

Even if they are taught in the finest schools imaginable by the best-paid teachers in the world, they will be deprived of the most precious possession a man can ever have, the faith that helps men live for God.

Obviously, if there are going to be strong families who keep hold of their children and train them in the fear of the Lord, the first group of people who must be aware of the problem of child stealing is the parents themelves.

Why are people willing to turn their children over to great community agencies when they know that these agencies are unable to teach their children the essential things they need to know, facts about God and about man, God's image bearer? Public educational institutions, for example, are allegedly based on a common-denominator religion which is supposed to satisfy everyone, but which in fact can never satisfy those who really believe in Jesus. Our public agencies are communicating what is essentially a state religion. How can people surrender their children, without a fight, to the great processes which are taking their children from beneath their control and placing them under the control of these massive institutions? The reason is frightening, but obvious: these people have no faith, no vital religion themselves. They are without conviction and at sea.

Is it possible that the main reason that you have been willing to surrender your children to others is that you have been afraid of them and you just haven't known what you should say to them? The only way that you can withstand the terrible pressures to relinquish your children to the broad community is this: your own life must be rooted and grounded in the Word of the living God, the Bible. Furthermore, you must believe its message of redemption through the

123

cross of the Lord Jesus Christ. And this Jesus must become your Lord. You must learn what it means to live a consistent Christian life, diligently trying to relate all of your activity to the Lordship of this Jesus.

If you believe on the Lord Jesus Christ yourself, this same Lord will give you His Holy Spirit so that you will be able to give your children the direction they need so desperately. They will naturally learn the basic elements of the true Christian life from you. As they see the role prayer plays in your life, they will naturally become praying children. Soon they too will learn that this life and our world cannot be understood without believing in God and living out of His Bible. Faith will come for them along natural lines and there will be a rapport between you and your children because you know that essentially you both believe the same thing and you are both on the same side.

If you have never thought much about this problem you must do some hard thinking before it is too late. God summons you to a living, useful faith in His Son. And then He calls you to train your children in the fear of the Lord. God says your children belong to you. That is why He says, "Children obey your parents in the Lord." He doesn't just want them to cut the grass when you say they should or carry out the garbage when you tell them to. He wants them to learn about Jesus from you.

Young people who are planning some day to be married and have a family are possibly the ones who are going to have to do something about the problem of child stealing. Many of you are pretty good fighters, and sometimes you can see through things better than the older generation.

Well, what about those children you hope to have

some day? How are you going to look at them? Will they just be the by-product of your marriage, and will you be glad to turn them over to public institutions? Wouldn't you like to have something to give your children, something big, important, like a magnificent set of values, a grand perspective, and a sensitive response to the mystery of living? Wouldn't you like to give them something like that?

Start as of right now to found your life upon God's Word, the Bible, so that Jesus Christ is your captain and your leader. That faith in Jesus is not the *in* thing right now doesn't make any difference. Remember that, without faith in Jesus, you will never be able to have a family that will be free of the domination of society. Without faith in Jesus, you'll *contribute* to our inevitable advance to all the 1984 horrors you know so much about.

You must believe in Jesus. You must believe His Word and find His people. And you must live out of that faith, not just in a church or chapel, but everywhere — in the laboratory, in front of your easel, in the classroom. When you start thinking about marriage, make sure that you find someone who shares your convictions about God and life and human destiny. Then take upon yourself the glorious, brave, faith-filled task of having children and living with them as God's representatives, so that when they come to you to find out what life is all about, you will be able to tell them like it is. And they will be able to obey you in the deepest, fullest sense of the word *obey* as they respond to your confession of faith with a confession of their own.

This child stealing within our culture is terribly serious, and you will be able to contribute to halting it in your life and in your family some day, if you start getting smart right now.

We should not be insensitive to the massive movement whereby parents abandon their responsibilities to bring up their children and public institutions take over the tasks the parents have laid aside. As the state assumes more and more of the responsibility for molding the children of the land, the great forces for personal freedom and liberty are gradually being squashed and a vast, uninteresting, monolithic society is beginning to take shape.

Don't let the state take *your* children away!

15

Our Intimate Enemies

An article called, "How to Make the Most of Family Fights," concludes with several rules designed to make family fights more useful than they generally are. Here are a few of the suggestions: "The main goal in a disagreement should be to reach a settlement which is mutually agreeable." Of course, that would be real nice, wouldn't it?

Another suggestion: "Disagreements should be discussed as calmly as possible between those in opposition." Agreed. But that's just the problem! How do you keep calm when you are fighting?

And then, another one is especially good: "Limit yourself. . . . Refrain from saying something during an argument that you'll be sorry about tomorrow. . . ." That's a good rule, too, but what the author fails to recognize is that this is precisely the problem. How does a person who is quarreling with someone else keep calm and refrain from saying something he will be sorry for tomorrow?

No, there's nothing too wrong with these rules, but when people get angry they don't always look at the rule book.

These kinds of rules are part of a new trend in family and marriage counseling which attempts to help people turn the most grim family and marriage problems into something constructive. It is a universal fact that husbands and wives frequently disagree absolutely, and the experience is often heart shattering for one or both of them. In addition to the occasions for disagreement between marriage partners, the total family situation compounds the problem. Parents find themselves reprimanding and even quarreling with their children. Brothers and sisters can really get at each other, too.

Today we are told that we should not necessarily think of family fights as good or bad. We must adopt a mature attitude about them and understand that they are inevitable expressions of natural human behavior. It is not in the spirit of our times to brand human behavior as either good or bad. Therefore, family quarrels are not necessarily good or bad, either. They just exist, and we must make the most of them.

This approach, understand, is not just a new *popular* approach to family fighting. No. It is buttressed by a new genre of scientific writings which insist on describing a man as an extension of the animal kingdom. Some time ago, both Konrad Lorenz and Robert Ardrey wrote books that argued that human aggression is an expression of animal instincts. Both books became best sellers and have contributed to the new invitation to make the most of family fights. A recent book, *The Intimate Enemy,* now provides marriage partners with a handbook that teaches them "How to fight fair in love and marriage." It shows "how couples who fight together stay together *if* they use the right fight techniques." It reveals "the differences between male and female fight styles, and more."

This is all very intriguing. But before you fall for it, don't forget where it comes from. This refusal to make an ethical judgment about family quarrels comes from a very naturalistic view of man that forgets that

128

man is a highly moral creation of God. Man, as a matter of fact, according to the Bible, is the image bearer of God who lives in the presence of God constantly. All of his activity is subject to God's judgment. Those who know the Bible cannot buy the growing feeling that the bickering that can go on within the family is neither good nor bad. It is bad, because it is an expression of our lack of sensitivity for one another, our selfishness, insecurity, and jealousy.

To be sure, every marriage is marred by disagreements and even quarreling, and every family becomes a battleground from time to time. But just because this kind of human behavior is prevalent, we should not conclude that it is wholesome. And it is the height of pride and smugness to suggest that, even if family fights are not the highest form of human behavior, we will still be able to make them useful through our cleverness. Let's not deceive ourselves.

The Bible rejects the naturalistic view of man that says we are just born fighters. In I John 4 we read something quite different: "Beloved, let us love one another; for love is of God, and he who loves is born of God and knows God." This means that the Christian faith and knowing God bring about a new style of life in which people learn what it means to live in love with other people. And that will have a profound effect upon the family.

Love is very practical. But do not make the mistake of thinking that when the Bible talks about love it is talking about sex. *Sex* is often possessive, destructive, and inconsiderate. *Love* is kind, selfless, considerate, concerned, sacrificial, and healing. One passage of the Bible describes love this way: "Love is, patient and kind; love is not jealous or boastful; it is not arrogant or rude. Love does not insist on its own way; it is not irritable or resentful; it does not rejoice at wrong, but rejoices in the right. Love bears all things, believes all things, endures all things" (I Corinthians 13:4-7). When you have that kind of love within a home the rough corners of human behavior are smoothed down. Situations that could easily lead to an explosion are avoided.

The way of life in a family where there is love like this will be expressed in a serious attempt toward mutual helpfulness. Conversations will be sincere, hearty, and thoughtful. There will be expressions of interest and concern in each other's projects and problems. The family members will be polite to each other. There will be laughter and song. Family quarrels will be infrequent. When they do occur, they will be resolved quickly with little damage.

But is it realistic in our times, when everybody is so busy and nervous, ever to expect that such a condition of love could ever exist in a family? Everybody knows that we have this thing called the generation gap that really complicates matters. Besides, there is this competition thing that filters down from the business world, to the school, and right into the home itself. Husbands and wives often become rivals, and children compete for their parent's attention. They don't give a care for anyone but themselves. No wonder the bleak reality of the prevalent conditions in our families has caused many to surrender to the naturalistic view of the family. Everybody knows that the family is a jungle just like everything else is, and the best you can do is make the most out of the fights that are bound to occur within it.

There *is* something rather unreal about expecting much from the role of love within the family today. It is impractical to expect that love will be generated along natural lines. The Bible never suggests that it will, either. We are told to love one another, but we are not told that human beings have a knack for loving. As a matter of fact, the Bible admits that we are entirely incapable of doing this ourselves. The only way we can live in love together is that we believe that God is love and that He has loved us totally and magnificently.

The Bible first tells us that we should love each other, but hastens to explain that this love can grow only out of our recognition that God has loved us in Jesus Christ, His only begotten Son, who died on Calvary so that unlovable, sinful men might have eternal life. In John's first letter we read, ". . . he who loves God is born of God and knows God. He who does not love does not know God for God is love. . . . In this is love, not that we loved God but that he loved us and sent his Son. . . . Beloved, if God so loved us, we also ought to love one another. . . . Whoever confesses that Jesus is the Son of God, God abides in him and he in God. So we know and believe the love God has for us. God is love, and he who abides in love abides in God, and God abides in him" (I John 4:7, 8, 10, 11, 15, 16).

When you start talking about a subject like this, you see just how much the Christian style of life differs from the naturalistic style of life that is becoming so prominent. Of course, if you don't believe in God and creation, and if you accept the theory that everything has evolved in one way or another from material, then you must look at your family as a step along the way in man's evolutionary development. There is no use getting too excited about whether the quarrels are right or wrong. Make the best of them, and may the fittest survive.

But the Bible's view of man is utterly different. And if your family is in big trouble right now, or your marriage is, perhaps you would do well to investigate the Bible's alternative to the modern naturalistic description of human behavior.

When you do that, you will see that the Bible reveals that God is deeply concerned about the structure and the health of the family. God wants it to be the place where the message of His grace is transmitted from the parents to their children. In Deuteronomy God commands His people to tell their children His words. He said, "And these words, which I command you this day shall be upon your heart; and you shall teach them diligently to your children . . ." (6:6, 7).

But the Bible does not consider the family only a place for instruction. The Bible also talks a great deal about the only thing that can make marriage and the family wonderful and holy. The Bible has been written so that those who know God will love Him and their neighbor. As a matter of fact, we are told repeatedly that love is the fulfillment of the entire law of God. (See Romans 13:8, 10; Galatians 5:14.)

Love can make the family a happy place to live. Love can smooth off the rough edges of disagreement and can cause reconciliation between a husband and wife. Children who observe Christian love in their parents begin to sense something of what it means to express love themselves. The Christian faith, if it is real and not just a formal cultural part of life, is accompanied by love. People who love each other will never look on their quarrels as just another instance of human aggression that we shouldn't get too excited about. Because they know what Christian love is they will strenuously avoid situations that they know will cause disagreement and tension. And when fighting

132

breaks out on the family front, they will do all they can to heal the ugly wounds as soon as possible.

There is no question about it, it is extremely difficult to express love in daily life. It is extremely hard to express love within the family, too. It is within our family that we find our intimate enemies. We know each other very well. We know how to make each other angry by remarks that might sound quite innocent to an outsider. Some days we do not feel as good as we do other days. We are often irritable. We see each other at our worst.

Therefore, when the Bible talks about love, it very frankly announces that there isn't going to be much love in the lives of those who reject God and His Christ. Remember, we read, "God is love." Men are not loving. Men are fighters. It is true; they are. But they are fighters, not because they are at a certain imperfect stage of evolutionary development; they are fighters because they have turned their backs upon their Creator and have insisted on denying His claim upon their lives. Man, created in the image of God, has descended to the hatred and animosity that uses up so much of his energy. That is why the family is a battleground so often.

Love becomes a possibility only for those who are united to God by faith. The Bible says, "Whoever confesses that Jesus is the Son of God, God lives in him, and he lives in God." That's the secret. Right there. Those who believe that Jesus is the Son of God are united to God, and God lives in them. And then, then only, they begin to live a life of love.

This has profound implications for family living. What about those people who claim to be Christians, but whose homes are full of tension and hatred? Some parents may be Christians, but they know about as much about love as they know about astro-navigation. Their children leave home as soon as they can because they cannot tolerate the lovelessness.

When you have Christian people who claim that God lives in them because they have faith in Jesus Christ, shouldn't you be able to sense the presence of love within their homes? Those who claim to be Christians may not rest until they have learned to live the life of love with those who could so easily become their most intimate enemies. And if they find it hard to be loving, they must pray fervently that God will bind them closer to Jesus through faith, so that the love of God will be expressed in their lives.

Even if you don't claim to be a Christian, this is important for you. What about your family? Or the family you hope to have some day? Have you swallowed the naturalistic view of man and of the family that teaches us not to get too excited about family fights and that suggests that we should just try to make the most of them? If that really is the best you can expect from your marriage and your home, it certainly isn't very much.

Perhaps you should seriously consider the Bible's total message about Jesus. The Bible says so clearly that He is the Son of God and that He died on the cross to take away the sins of all those who believe in Him. This means that if you believe in Him, you can possess the love that alone can bring a ray of light into your dreary life. Maybe your family is a shambles right now. You don't know Christ, and the rest of your family doesn't either. *This* is the reason there is no love in your home: you have never believed in God who is love and you have rejected the greatest gift of His love, Jesus, who died so that sinners just like you and me could be set on the road of love ourselves.

This all points to just one thing. Jesus Christ is the most important Person in all the world. Once again, we learn that without Jesus, human life keeps moving downhill — down, down, down, to the bitter point where all love is finally extinguished. People are talking about the extinction of the family as we know it. It's inevitable, really. Only those who know Jesus and who trust in Him receive power to live in love in that most delicate, intricate, and intimate of human situations: the family.

Only Jesus can save you and your family. Only Jesus can give you the strength to love those who can so easily become your most intimate enemies.

16

The Greatest Song

"The song of love is a sad song. . . ." That is certainly true. The song of love is the saddest song man has ever sung, especially today. I mean the song that describes the relationships between men and women, the song of sexual love. How twisted it has grown!

In St. Louis, Dr. Masters has spent the last few years investigating the subject with clinical detachment. Standing in Kinsey's tradition he has collected a great quantity of data that has made us more knowledgeable concerning sex than ever before. And married people may take their problems to St. Louis and Dr. Masters will help them there.

But if some have misgivings about Masters' deceptively austere approach to sex in St. Louis, there should be outrage about the general deterioration of human feelings concerning human sexuality. Obviously we are in bad trouble. Mankind has become obsessed with his body. That in itself would not be catastrophic, except that man thinks of his body almost exclusively as a scaffold that supports his sex. Other than that, the body is despised, even ruined.

Men are apparently near bewilderment about their sexuality, but there is a rawness about the bewilderment that leaves us reeling. The most intimate of human relationships is now depicted with a jolting realism that leaves nothing to the imagination. Once our children have reached the ripe old age of eighteen and can prove it they become eligible to witness the most explicit movies of sex and perversion. And the rancid sex books that clog the bookstores and ride high on the top of best seller lists depict a sexuality that is joltingly animal.

So then, if the song of love was ever sad, it is incredibly so today. It seems now as if the possibility of a meaningful, joy-filled relationship between a husband and wife has been scuttled completely. People are hopelessly hung up on sex — everybody. There is no class that is immune to this sickness. People are stumbling over their sexuality as never before.

The ugliness of the modern perverted view of sexuality gets to us in hundreds of ways that fall far short of dull witted pornography. Some of the most popular women's magazines are just as sex-drenched as *Playboy*. In a different way, of course, but they are thoroughly devastating, for they sneak up on respectable women folk and make them quite lascivious. The perverted view of sexuality dominates much advertising. A perverted view of sexuality dominates the field of fashion where to be well dressed means to be dressed in a sexually attractive way. The flap over the disappearance of the miniskirt is another display of the overriding interest in this subject. Modesty has gone out of style long ago.

The damage that is being caused by the unholy perversion of the song of love is widespread. The young people who make headlines because they sometimes go bathing in the nude in reflecting pools or insist that coeducation should extend to the college dormitory are not the only ones who pervert the song of love. Their very fathers and mothers do not have a happy record either when it comes to these things. Just ask the ministers in your community where the trouble lies today, and if they are honest, they will probably say, "Everywhere." The perverted sexual interests of people today have distorted beyond recognition the greatest song of all, the song of love between a husband and wife, a wife and husband, warm and full and satisfying, within the sacred bonds of marriage.

Jesus talked about love, too, and we should listen to His message. "You shall love the Lord your God with all your heart, . . ." He said, "[and] you shall love your neighbor as yourself" (Matthew 22:37, 39). We must focus on this statement in order to lift ourselves out of the ugly mess we are in regarding love and sex. For when Jesus says, "love your neighbor as yourself," He demands that first of all we get that nearest, most intimate of all love relationships straightened out so that it is good and wholesome. For the man whose love for his wife is coarse and meaningless and interrupted by unfaithfulness, and the woman whose love for her husband has grown cold, can really only play at loving others. They cannot do what Jesus says they must do.

It may surprise you, but the Bible that summarizes all of the commands of God in terms of love, allows us to speak realistically and meaningfully about the love that graces holy wedlock. If the song of love has been a terribly sad song in your life, you should read the book that elevates love to its heights. In the history of translations it has often been called *The Greatest Song*. Perhaps in yours it is called the *Song of Solomon*.

The Greatest Song, found just after the Book of Proverbs in the Scriptures, has long been a riddle. It is obviously an exalted poem and its rhythm is infectious and its imagery rich. But it is, strangely, apparently about the love of a man and a woman and it is cast in straightforward, physical language. Thus, it has been an embarrassment to Christian people throughout the years. But this embarrassment has arisen from a kind of non-Biblical prudishness. And when you begin to see that the Bible is not burdened with the self-consciousness we feel about the body, the message of the Song of Songs becomes gloriously liberating. Especially today, when we are making such utter fools of ourselves in terms of our sexuality, the message of the Song of Songs, or the Song of Solomon, is needed desperately. And it is needed also when we talk about what Jesus Christ of Nazareth meant when He said that we are to love our neighbor as ourselves.

The book of the Bible that we have come to call the Song of Songs, or the Song of Solomon, is hard to understand under the best of circumstances. But it is even harder to understand because followers of Jesus have been reluctant to deal with it openly and in a straightforward manner. For centuries there was an unwillingness to admit that the book should be received literally within the church, and so it was considered by many to be a long figure of speech that illustrated the love Christ had for His people. But an open-minded, uncluttered reading of it in today's world shows very clearly that this exuberant book is about the love a man and a woman can have for each other within marriage. It is chastely erotic, and this chaste eroticism is desperately needed today.

God, who created man, created him male and female, and thus, with the infinite wisdom of His divine intelligence, He laid the reality of sexuality into the very fabric of human relationships. But it was and is an aspect of human life that is finally expressed most fully and in a most God-honoring way when it results in a man and a woman becoming one flesh within

139

marriage. So, at the risk of being boringly obvious, it is necessary to underscore that sex has been made by God on purpose for the betterment of our lives. The holy book, the Song of Solomon, presupposed the goodness of our sexuality as it can be expressed within marriage when it heralds the exalted quality of faithful love. If there is a key statement at all, it is found in chapter 2:16 which states: "My beloved is mine and I am his. . . ." It is this overriding faithfulness and singleness of love's focus that emerges from the Song of Songs.

Professor Calvin Seerveld of Trinity Christian College has provided a rich interpretation of this book, and many who have read it and have seen the glorious operetta made from his work have been greatly helped by what he has done. In his view, the Song of Solomon furnishes us with a contrast between the sensual sexuality of the oriental harem and the pure, single-minded love of a lowly maiden and her shepherd lover. In so many ways the Bible's message is the Song of Songs can help us today.

When you think about it, the lustful wantonness that was found when kings had harems is very present today. The widespread divorce and unfaithfulness of the present is probably not so much a practice of serial polygamy as it is an expression of the fact that men want, down deep, to be able to view all women as available, as members of their potential harem. The harem idea is very powerful and though harems are few, men feel it their right to cast their lustful glances everywhere, and women, apparently, achieve a kind of strange satisfaction in being a member of the mini-skirted harem.

In the Book of the Song of Solomon, or the Song of Songs, the harem idea is discarded and the maiden expresses her devoted love in the simple statement that "My beloved is mine and I am his. . . ." With relentless determination she wards off the advances of the monarch who claims his rights as her master, and returns with resolute affection to her lover. "My beloved is mine and I am his, he pastures his flock among the lilies. Until the day breathes and the shadows flee, turn, my beloved, be like a gazelle, or a young stag upon rugged mountains" (2:16, 17).

The Song of Songs finally concludes with the victory of the faithful love of the maiden and her shepherd lover. The eighth chapter of the book is a soaring song of heartrending gladness as the faithful maid is reunited with her lover and the degrading, grotesque love of the harem is exchanged for the purity of the love that can flow between a man and a woman in marriage. Within the framework of this holy description of faithful, chaste, sexual love the Song of Songs presents an unself-conscious expression of total, free, unhindered delight in the physical aspects of this pure love.

Love your neighbor as yourself, and Jesus invites us to exercise this first of all in terms of our marriages. There is no person closer to us than our mate. Love, according to the Song of Songs, can be changed from a sad song into the greatest song by those who exercise it along with the most profound respect for the person who is the object of their love. The destructive, animal quality of so much of that which is called love today is rooted in a faulty view of man and woman. They become objects who excite each other and that is that. Within the Bible a man is sacred and a woman is, too, and when they are united in marriage, the resulting union is sacred. It must be preserved and maintained at all costs.

There is no question that the Bible clearly exalts the

love for a man and a woman within marriage. Those who know their Bible well know that in the earliest years the Bible reports polygamy as rather common among the people of God. And some of the kings of Israel had many wives, as did all the great monarchs in those ancient days. But when Christ comes and the people of God are filled with the Holy Spirit, the Bible explicitly and repeatedly holds up the marriage of one man to one wife as the great ideal. And in terms of this ideal all the richness of human sexuality is to be experienced.

The song of love is a sad song. How true, and how tragic! But the song of love can become the song of songs for a husband and wife who together know God and His Son, the Lord Jesus Christ. Within the bonds of their sacred relationship they can begin to obey Jesus' commandment: "You shall love your neighbor as yourself."

Yet not everyone is married. True. But the possibilities within marriage for two people finding one another and helping one another wonderfully are exceptionally important for our modern world. For if marriage finally deteriorates and lust displaces love everywhere, catastrophe will overtake us. For some, the grand ideal held out by the Song of Songs in the Bible is a goal toward which they move. They are the young people who want to be pure and holy so that they will be able to experience the fulness of the married love the Song of Songs tells us about. For some, this grand ideal will always remain unrealized within their life for one reason or another. Yet, for them too, the very presence of this possibility within our world is a source of inspiration. For some, the ideal of holy married love is now a memory as they are called on to advance alone — the widows and the widowers. Yet the memory of their joy can sustain them and encourage them even now.

But there are many of us who *are* married right now or who will be very soon. For us, the command of Jesus to love our neighbor as ourselves must be honored first within our marriages. There love can be experienced and expressed in mysterious fulness. For there it can be said, "My beloved is mine and I am his."

Our perverted sexuality is the proof of our rebellion against God. Let each of us confess his sin and failure and return to Jesus Christ, the Son of God, and obey His holy commandments. Then the song of love that has become so unutterably sad could well become the song of songs for us.